SIDEBROW BOOKS

THE YESTERDAY PROJECT

Published by Sidebrow Books
P.O. Box 86921
Portland, OR 97286
sidebrow@sidebrow.net
www.sidebrow.net

Cover art by Tyler Bewley
Cover & book design by Jason Snyder

ISBN: 1-940090-04-0
ISBN-13: 978-1-940090-04-7

FIRST EDITION | FIRST PRINTING
9 8 7 6 5 4 3 2 1
SIDEBROW BOOKS 015
PRINTED IN THE UNITED STATES

Sidebrow Books titles are distributed by
Small Press Distribution

Titles are available directly from Sidebrow at
www.sidebrow.net/books

A Member of
inter
section
incubator
Services for Artists
www.theintersection.org

Sidebrow is a member of the Intersection Incubator, a program of
Intersection for the Arts (www.theintersection.org) providing fiscal
sponsorship, incubation, and consulting for artists. Contributions
to Sidebrow are tax-deductible to the extent allowed by law.

THE YESTERDAY PROJECT

BEN DOLLER & SANDRA DOLLER

SIDEBROW BOOKS + 2016 + PORTLAND & SAN FRANCISCO

for Ronald Johnson, 2005-2015

ONE

Yesterday we woke up to vegan food over Mendo. Over the fog coast and ran into Sid on the way in, who said, I'm only the kitchen manager. But he is so much more. Bought his book on the way out, *Approaching the Natural*. So it was like running into natural, running into an approach. The hostess sat us, a skinny grump. You had the view of the redwoods, I had the view of the people. Which is natural. Lots of children with eyes and everybody is somebody's daughter. What a perfect daughter you have, somebody said to someone else. The one table with two unbelonging, the woman much happier to see her woman than to see her child. The one little boy in a green hoodie carted off screaming, But I don't want to go. I say it's difficult when you get language and are able to say what you want and more importantly what you don't want even as it is happening to you. He walks out small behind his mother of his own free will hollering about how I don't want to go. That was breakfast with cashew sauce and polenta and kale which I thought was spinach but you told me was dino kale.

Yesterday you drove us up into Mendocino to the pipe shop over the hill and under the feather trees. I walked with my bum knee on the cobbles and we got a tour of the glass blown into bowls for the perfect smoke. The energetic hippie wouldn't stop. An old folks walked in, lured by the ceramic cups in the window that you told me are for keeping your stash. I just thought it was bait & switch, smart hippies. The old folks took one look and left. Later I saw them crossing another street holding hands, all beige and crochet and wooden buttons and not buying weed pipes for later or for their grandkids like I'd hoped.

There was another impromptu gathering of happy old women in the bookstore. This is the place to come for old women. If you die and leave me old alone, I'm moving here with my knitteds. But remind me not to put up a sign about my Russian-English speaking dog who needs a play date, someone will write how arrogant and that will be the end of that.

Yesterday we bought socks. For $15.99, $12.99, and $9.00. There were no cheap slippers so we got some wool, some bamboo, some hemp wear for our tootsies. I drove us back after reading Mark's and Emily's and Chad's and Barb's and my mother's emails on the phone in the car in front of the co-operative in the old church.

Then the sun came out and vitamin D3 was possible and we all lay in it on the deck over the river—we two and the two dogs—as if it had been months since seen. After lentil soup with carrots, kale, cabbage, potatoes, yam and a flavor tray, we walked them up the hill with brush all around, curling around the lip of the river where the RVs park. One happy white dog in a boat below. One enormous malamute approaches. My bum knee. I try to convince you how unusual and chic I would be, a girl with a limp. I wear pleated high-waist jeans you found for me, rolled up over my black boots with a black X t-shirt and a black & white polka-dotted sweater.

Later we read and wrote and had a glass of wine with the quinoa and broccoli you made. There was no TV, no movies. I did Ashtanga primary series on the deck. I read Maria Damon on the margins and Sarah Bay-Cheng on Gertrude Stein. Poets are the only scholars. You read Ben & Feliz & Brett and Harry Mathews. I researched adoption and saw photos of unwanted children I didn't want to see.

I forgot about our morning bath together in the profound clawfoot and washing my hair with African black soaps and you rinsing it and trying to figure how to build me the same setup, the faucet I can control from within the bath, without standing. I forgot about the long night, how I woke up thinking about your cancer and how will we know if it's come back and when and what are the chances and why do they keep talking about three-year, five-year survival, and what is the mark. When will I know if you've survived.

07.17.2014

Yesterday arrived, we didn't yet have this plan. We had another plan: go to the Raven restaurant and try the vegan biologique health breakfast here in Mendo. We are on vacation and the kitchen is tough to work in, and we are healing, and we are here. We went there. But first we woke up. I woke up first, two hours before I woke you up, and I read almost 70 pages of Harry Mathew's *My Life in CIA*, kind of a record for me—I am feeling this vacation—it's a page-turner, and I started to tell you about it when I woke up, but when you asked if we could read it together I didn't want to read it anymore.

So we drove to the Raven, it was farther than I thought, but I knew it was on the right and it was. Eco-lodge chic, not really chic at all, just wood everywhere, probably indigenous redwood paneling not in the reclaimed variety we see so often in San Diego, more the hunting club kind that betrays no gesture towards hipness. Which is what is cool about it up here, and I'm glad you had the idea to drive up. It's also always chilly, and we needed supplies from the town. You were underwhelmed by your polenta, you're in the quest for never-ending vegetables because you want me to live.

I think we've been to the town before, but when we talk about it, we can't remember, though I think I convinced you then you convinced me, now I'm not really sure, but we've been to a few towns like this before, we keep comparing, Hudson NY, Canandaigua NY, Ithaca NY, most of coastal Oregon, hippie towns with water, co-ops and fog. We did the walking tour. I loved the way you were happy. We went into a shop with beautiful pottery and glasswork for smoking marijuana. The owner was so nice! I didn't know there existed both a decorative glass industry and a functional glass industry. I didn't know that bongs and bowls could sell for five thousand. We bought the Panda. He cost $40. We bought some notebooks elsewhere that cost almost $20 each. We were really vacationing now. We went to a store just for socks. $40! We walked by the music festival. Music escaped the tent. We went to the co-op in the church. $70—much on my favorite nut butter famous for healing adopted nutrient-deficient children.

I hope I heal. You are doing everything you can. But there is an air of eulogy in the way you Google our prospective adoptive children. I saw you doing yoga on the deck, the ten minutes the sun were out, when my P90x3 was over. I can't believe what you are capable of. I tried to do the moves behind you, me your big lumbering shadow. My anklebone couldn't take the pressure.

We walked R & K and saw a man with a huge malamute. Luckily, I had both dogs because of your bum knee. The dogs freaked out, but not too bad.

I wanted to do it with you all day, but we hugged a lot instead. It was a busy day. We wrote for an hour in our separate rooms, some project I started about writing a book called *Book*. We'll see. We had soup and later quinoa with broccoli and beets and potatoes from the pressure cooker. When I thought I turned the pressure cooker off, I turned it up. When I thought I double-checked, I turned the other burner on high, without lighting it (it's an antique Wedgewood). Fumes set off the fire alarm, and I waved my iPad at it to turn it off. I could have killed us all.

JULY 18, 2014

Yesterday yesterday started. Movement in the bed, chronological. Fast morning and warm tea, getting colder in the carafe. A new project, a reality show. Each day, a performance of living. Each record, a matter. This is what it's like to be here.

In college there was a younger girl with attention problems who made a photography art project called "This is what it's like in here" showing how sad it was to be her, sad little negligee and fake blood and sorry eyes. I always hated that line, that direction, that girl. Pity the animal.

This is what. Westerns with Joseph Cotton and Gary Cooper and the Preston Sturges actor who survived. No popcorn. Raw goji berry chocolate pieces. Cauliflower steak and tofu steak and wild rice and spinach salad. Lentil soup. Egg frittata with red peppers. Flavor tray. Gertrude Stein and Maria Damon. Bob Kauffman. Fanny Howe at the end of it all, her wild childhood now in pieces.

I emailed the doctor who didn't get the slides of your original lesion, no word on the real diagnosis, no word on.

The meditation walk over the cliff over the sea, which we couldn't see for the crying out fog. A roost of buzzards behind the Ledford Inn. Silent walking and pointing. When we walk the dogs in silent, the world makes the walk. Many men in trucks pulled over eating sandwiches and burritos, not looking at us, not looking at anything. Thanks for the break. Each man in his own truck alone.

Except for one truck with seven dogs and a living woman. She comes chasing after us asking if her dogs can play with our dogs. I don't care if they bite mine, she says, I don't care. I wouldn't have gotten another dog, but he's her son you see. He's part pit bull and lab. Look how much they want to play. She says as they rip at their lines and snarl and lash and teeth and super fun. She is like me but wearing crocs. I'm wearing pebble-print skinny jeans, my bone-print black sweatshirt, the new GBV "cool earth tour" pink tee, the Parisian wooly scarf with the holes, a red hoodie, black ankle moto boots. New socks. I think about this.

Two hot baths yesterday and oil. Some painful writing. Painful is the name of the Western town Gary Cooper and his half-wit ride into with the wrong initials, MJ, Melody Jones. Why does Gary Cooper take himself so unseriously. Why does he look so much like Tom Beller.

Yesterday my sisters and their sisters and brothers scattered the ashes of their original mother into the lake in upper Washington. I think this happened, but I have no proof.

Yesterday you transcribed and I inscribed some more, for what. The sound of your typing was maddening and I wrapped up my little pink dog in a wooly blanket. You had Ronald Johnson and I had Kiki Smith and that was a reversal.

I saw the mugs of my dream in the store, small and bright with no handles, matte not shiny, monochrome. We didn't buy them. We ate our soup from Lucite green mugs on the back deck over the river where the people still stay in their RVs, never come out. Larger and larger birds with red beaks flew by us on their way down, some white birds circled the river bank and the RVs. You call them all eagles though they are hawks or falcons or buzzards or swoops.

In the end I was nauseous and wished I had slept through another Western. I made new water and washed our glasses and cut new pieces of lemon and lime, lemon for you and lime for me. I wished it was over in my stomach. I slept through. Dreamt that one of Matt and Scarlett's sons had died and it was awful. Fell asleep reading Fanny and her record of everything. She continues to get smaller and more entire. Lullaby for adulthood.

07.18.2014

Yesterday was here. We started this. Write a page in the morning, side by side, you're always faster. You lap me right away.

Then I walked around this rented house, made tea. Yesterday I made eggs scrambled with a million vegetables: mushrooms, kale, tomatoes, pepper, shallot, garlic. I cleaned up after the dogs. Yesterday I read a collaborative book written by Ben and Brett and Feliz.

I loved their book, and not—I think—because of our scholarly association, our friendship, or the way it feeds my ego. It doesn't feed my ego. It makes me feel incompetent, their quick brains, their humor, their dramas. I can barely remember what happened yesterday. I can see how their project, writing letters to Wes Anderson, overlaps with this one, maybe is even what got us doing this (although this was your idea), also how entirely different it is.

Later we were walking the dogs on an unknown trail, nearby across the highway. You said we should try walking meditation. I think that is what walking is, if there's no talking involved. But you have to commit to meditation.

We were on some bluffs, hard to see the water with all the mist. The dogs could feel our commitment. They are always meditating. You nodded towards two vultures (kinda breaking the code of meditation ethics) but I appreciated it. Vultures are as big as eagles, but get no respect because of their carrion tendencies. They're just freegans. They should be America's official bird, America's or California's.

It was peaceful, but every ten feet the seclusion broken by a worker in a truck eating a sandwich. It was getting harder to meditate. Perhaps the vultures get their crusts. After three of those trucks, there was another kind of truck, a homeless truck, a truck that was more for sleeping and storage. An explosion of angry dog voices, R & K broke their meditation and joined in. Kiki was wearing her pink hoodie with her collar attached through a slit in the back. She was mine. She was straining at her collar, choking herself, almost losing it, but she wasn't the worst dog in this kennel.

There was a dog under the truck, fierce, teeth everywhere. I didn't know how you could be handling Ronald with your bum knee. But I think our meditative states kept the dogs more level than usual, not plugged in to our usual anxiety. We made it past the feral truck and dogs.

Past more workers, some doing some work.

To a winding path that went down a hill, with warning signs promising doom if we kept going.

There was a crazy lady's voice behind us, but we had to go back. She was at the crest of the hill in her crocs and nightgown, she was a crazy lady.

She wanted to have a doggy playdate. She didn't care if our dogs bit her dogs, she said. We dragged our dogs by her dogs, politely declined over and over.

Later I cooked cheddar cauliflower steaks and tofu steaks. The cheddar is the color of this crazy crucifer. It was a real success. We tried out the Panda and watched a Western with Gary Cooper, a kind of comedic one where he has no skills and a sidekick but is mistaken for a quick gun badass. Gary Cooper, Cary Grant, Clark Gable. My friends.

Yesterday was not one thing. Walks in twos and threes and silence. A naked worker with an orange cap clearing vines on the hillside. Or a shirtless squatter with an orange helmet gathering berries and bed stuff. I saw a smashed dead snake worm-sized that you did or did not see. I stopped writing so fast. I concentrated on the non-project. Doing yoga on the deck teaches you to ignore people.

Yesterday I had an insecurity. Our waitress at the Italian grotto was an Anna Joy look-alike or sound-alike or spirit-alike and she shepherded us just the same. Lulled into dolce vita. That's what relationships are for, she said, sharing spaghetti. Or something.

Yesterday there was more no news about the Malaysian plane shot down. Yesterday I got more melanoma alerts that may or may not apply to you. Yesterday we both received 1-minute voice mails from Dr. Brouha. Neither message came through because we are in the sticks by the river. We will forget to call him back on Monday. You will forget to stay alive. I will have to remember to keep you alive.

No sun.

We walked by the Skunk Train to see if it was something we would do. Ride into the redwoods by old growth and understory, all poetic sorts of names for plants and flowers I'll forget. Ride like it was 1892.

We walked by the North Coast Brewery. The art deco poster of Thelonious' brew made us both want one. Why a Belgian, Dutchess, that's a lot of rubies. We peered in the bar windows at places we used to go. The fast-moving bar maid grabbed another six-pack from the cooler. A teenage girl with long brown legs tried to cross the street to her laughing car of friends. Their laughter seemed incommensurate with the task.

Yesterday I was too serious. On the way home I lunked inside my womanish lot. Care is an oppressive word. I tried to look at the lights behind the Victorian windows on the crests or the bluffs or whatever they call them. I looked into the trees.

It rained on me on the yoga deck. A working neighbor played Phil Collins' one good song. I only took one bath. I wanted to get inside my Turkish robe so quickly I forgot to dry off my hair. It hung in brown wet strings around my face. You took my picture with my hood on, a boxer. You started taking pictures. You read actual things while I read about things. You read David Byrne and told me about it. We wrote in our separate rooms.

It wasn't yesterday we bought pots and pans and strainers and popcorn from the store. Yesterday we bought cans of dog food and dry dog food and rawhides. Wild boar food. Yesterday I made tea. I am aware this sounds depressing. This is all part of it.

You are typing faster than I am. You are probably writing about one or two important incidents. I am trying to capture some movement. I just coughed and the sound was interruptive. The truth is I don't remember yesterday at all, don't even want to. Something about an antique refrigerator, trying to keep the tea warm all day, making water, making a vegetable smoothie, throwing out the rice from the day before, making plans to see a movie then not seeing a movie, watching Joanne Woodward and Henry Fonda con a poker game. You are probably writing about that. It's official, I am colonized. This is the worst idea.

07.19.2014

Yesterday we woke up, we typed the last day up. I don't know how it will go, if I will reveal anything at all. I don't know what the audience is, not that that ever mattered, but now thinking this form of address, the wonky pronoun stuff that happens. There was tea. If everything follows form, your half will keep mine afloat, just like this life we call ours.

We both had messages on our iPhones from my dermatologist, Brouha. But we're out of range, and there was just the message that there was a message, each 50 seconds long, neither of which we could access. Maybe they have my scans? By the time we were in range to call, later yesterday, it was the weekend.

You made breakfast: leftover polenta and lots of vegetables. It tasted fantastic. We are finally learning to feed ourselves in this new era. Anno Cancero. I thought so much, yesterday, about our luck, our bounty, the fact that we can be somewhere, mostly typing, mostly eating, walking our dogs in this weird Northern California land where the sun never comes out, how lucky we are to complain about it.

Every day we take our supplements, my two reishi, six spirulina, multi-vitamin, 5,000-mg vitamin D, CoQ10, flax oil, curcumin. You take smaller bits of the same.

It is so generous of you to swallow all the pills too—I can dry swallow anything, golfballs, but you take them one at a time, a few less than I do.

You have no sugar, no caffeine, no animals, no booze, no gluten. Your solidarity is astonishing. I filled your water glass halfway through your pills.

It takes a while to get going when you're in the Creative Class, you made smoothies at some point, and I read accessible books while you read difficult ones. I read a bunch of *How Music Works*, kind of shuttling backwards through it. Byrne's brain is so historical, something about the Bo Diddley beat osmosified into rock and roll via Mexico via Mississippi. I thought along with David Byrne about the economy of Pop, of Pop as an art form whose most aesthetic elements are located in its calculations. We finished my soup.

I think I took two baths yesterday. I did my agility training. I sweat like a giant wound. You were doing headstands on the deck. My scar hurt when I was jumping, I wondered if I was dying.

We walked the dogs. I saw a worker working in the bushes. You saw a naked vagrant in the bushes. The dogs pooped at a Corgi crossing. Scottie? You'll remember.

Yesterday, body parts were scattered everywhere. We drove up the coast a bit in the evening, there was even some sun. We went to Fort Bragg. We couldn't walk on the coast there: there were toxicity warnings. It reminded me of home.

We had a lovely, expensive dinner. Everything is organic here, we've decided. We contemplated the Skunk Train while we waited for our movie. Two middle-aged (my-aged?) men played acoustic guitars. One of them butchered his lead. You said this is nice. I made an exaggerated "really?" face. It was supposed to be a mock judgment of his bad note but it seemed to condemn our whole situation. We were both a little shocked at my ability to be just between us in public. I apologized to you, to the air. No one else saw me.

We skipped the movie. Drove back and had a little fight. Fights are so much sadder now. You thought I would hit a man walking beside the road. I thought I wouldn't. Neither of us can bring ourselves to bring it. You said I called you crazy. I said you were imagining things. The kind of gendered response that ruins the world.

We all got on a twin bed, you, me, R & K, and escaped into two escapist Westerns: *Stagecoach* and *Big Hand for the Little Lady*. Highly recommended.

JULY 20, 2014

Yesterday Wes Anderson was Fred MacMurray with Barbara Stanwyck, Stanny, in a pushed back cowgirl cap and floating trousers over high-heel boots tracking the wild cat. Stanny just had to have her houndstooth coat on a stick and then back on her shoulders. The crime killed her horse so she took another one with longer hair, not a moment missed. Stanny in blonde curls and a negligee turns up Stanny full makeup in the barn in an overcoat. Old films is understanding old women. Why sure.

Also in LA, Feliz and Ben and Brett read last night at the Poetic Research Bureau from *The Wes Letters*. To Wes Anderson. You read the book this week and read it to me or read it for me. I turn to odd pages where Feliz is finishing an imaginary letter and forgetting to sign it from Wes, and Ben is burying himself in Wes Anderson's front yard, but not dead, just buried. Brett is proliferating. They play a drinking game called Wes Anderson and win.

Yesterday Wes Anderson died and Fred MacMurray narrated it himself, attended his own funeral so to speak. They hanged a fastidious hobo moon-lighting as Wes Anderson. Wes Anderson was bad. Stanny holds the torch for Wes for five years—David Bowie—but then takes up with his brother, the dully named Tom. Tom wants in on the job at the bank, and then Tom dies. Tom gets shot with the tiniest pistol by his boss who has just fired him the day before. You rarely see people get fired in old films, it seems contemporary.

Five years is the time they give for recurrence. As if in five years everyone falls dumb dead from the disease.

At first, Stanny is mad at Wes for leaving, for moonlighting, for criming it up. Then she's mad at him for getting Tom killed. Then she gets deputized, gets her own little star, which she sashes to her hip in those chic crepe pants. She rides off to bring Wes Anderson in. Wes Anderson is hiding out cooking steaks in a cabin past the waterfall in the woods. His pardner holds him up and takes the cash, oversized packets of dollars. I've got enough dollars to buy a steak, so cook me a steak.

We walk the dogs by the river. As if I've never seen mosquitoes before. An old truck route and many versions of birds with naturalist names I won't say. A neighbor with a white truck had an old avocado farm in Fallbrook, he has to say "ex" wife.

Stanny and the crook have a shootout behind some rocks. This is where her houndstooth coat comes in. She makes it through the waterfall once and finds her man to take him in. Then gender remembers itself and restablizes, can you read it. The waterfall falls her after his warning, Wes Anderson is always right. Stanny falls terribly down the fall. Wes lassos her in and they make it back to the cabin, where Stanny admits everything was all her fault and if she had only loved him better, less strongly, less aggressively, Wes Anderson never would have left.

I have a natural resistance to writing the word aggressive. We have a fight I won't write about, you say some things not fit for print or film. I try to knock you off the waterfall.

If I have another bite of venison I'll grow horns.

07.20.2014

Yesterday the project settled in, not the writing, not the quality, but the rhythm, the waking and the typing, the tea. I used to drink two pots of coffee before I could speak a sentence.

We did the project, detailing yesterday's yesterday. Paul McCartney is everywhere in this, Ham and Eggs on the scratch track, substitution.

Meditation is my medication. We tried the Qigong your colleague dropboxed us. We were on Mars, the red energy was flowing into my heart from the tip of my tongue. K barked loudly and I couldn't get the word I was supposed to say. I asked you, it was "Coo." We cracked up, I had to stop the flight.

I discovered how to make a decent smoothie: all the superfoods all lined up: the maca, the cacao, the hemp hearts, the berries, the grass powder, the chia seeds, the flax seeds—that's the base, you save the vegetables for salads, because vegetables taste good the way they are.

Here's a good recipe for a smoothie: 1-2 cups of a combination of coconut milk and coconut water, 1 peach, 1/8 avocado, 1 Medjool date, all the superfoods. Blend 'til smooth. Add 2 cups of ice.

We drank our smoothies in the only sun of the day. Something about yesterday's project had made you sad. The world had become about me, and I've been encouraging it. We had an adult conversation. I listened and I understood.

I think I forgot to take my supplements yesterday!

We went on a hike! Drove the dogs to a park, which was a beach, and we walked the estuary. It was very beautiful. There are so many kinds of Westerns, the dust bowls, the gold panners, the different landscapes that the films were really about. Here's the kind where gold and logs are the currency, where water is everywhere.

It's in the air, in the constant haze that hangs here. We drove back in and saw that, one mile down the road, it breaks.

We saw that before though, on our hike—we saw the paddlers and canoeers skimming the estuary. We didn't see much wildlife but for mosquitos. They swarmed R, not really K. They attacked the black dog with the long hair. We forgot to bring water, we forgot to bring the dog's vests with their water packs—back at home. We forgot to bring the dog's life vests for aquatic fun— back at home. We forgot to bring our paddleboards—back at back at. We didn't even know where we were going and yesterday we finally got there.

I know why. Everything is your responsibility, and I've done nothing. It doesn't always work this way. Yesterday I loaded the page for Facebook, instinctively, then I closed the computer.

Yesterday I made tempeh sandwiches, pesto later. I am cooking up a tidal wave in this borrowed kitchen, in bloody rivalry with the healing restaurants nearby.

Yesterday I wondered if this project will reveal my shallowness, my shame, our fundamental imbalance, your great goodness, your good greatness.

We saw one good Western (Barbara Stanwyck and Fred MacMurray reprising their *Double Indemnity* role—Fred's character was named Wes Anderson), 1/5 of the worst one ever made (from the '90s/Jeff Bridges/ Wild Bill), and a truly great John Ford one whose name I forget. I kept falling asleep, but I read the synopsis earlier.

JULY 21, 2014

Yesterday is becoming a kind of trauma.

I was hostess to a Helen I'll never meet. Here's where to find the ironing board, the hammer, the hairdryer. Did I leave enough champagne. When you think of KG is it Kevin Garnett or Kendall Grady. This tells you where you are.

We started with forbidden breakfast. Apricot scone and everything bagel and lox platter, green twiggy tea and cappuccino. The small chubby boy in the striped tank top chased away the birds on the bench. He chased away the birds until he was in the street. The women behind us, one gray, one brass, talked about their older sex lives. Give Phil a try, you never know, maybe he has sex in his dreams. At first the elder was talking about being a revolutionary in Chicago in '68, getting arrested, Cambodia, and then Israel. Every woman they mentioned, they mentioned her age. Rose, who's 82. My Aunt Mary Alice, who's in her 80s. Paradise for old women is no paradise at all.

Walked the headlands and saw an alpaca. You said, I'm so glad we came here. I'm so glad you said that, happy summer camp for we. We didn't even know where we were going. I just picked a spot on the map and we came here. Who knew we would be surrounded. Alpacas and organic markets and books and river and sea both. I didn't even know there would be water.

Should all people be artists if it means peppering the world with more and more dog art and gold wire representation. People like to sell their art in booths at fairs. I wanted that one ceramic mug but how to get it home and was it really that different from the other ceramic mugs elsewhere. It was there.

An older couple, he walks behind her with his hand in her back pocket holding on like child. She smiles. Is there something wrong or is this just their situation.

Lots of Joe Brainard and his masculine notations. Lots of male in Joe. Joe at 19, Joe at 26. At 26 Joe worries about being old. How many Joes live here now, actual old. Joe writes about smoking four packs a day. That's it. He makes a good point about how cancer doesn't get you tomorrow, it takes years and who cares. I guess it's tomorrow.

Yesterday woodwork and the massage and the bath and I figured out how to sleep in a braid so my hair doesn't strangle me in the night. You went out to get mushrooms but came back with a paper bag of sprouts, pea sprouts, and sprouted adzukis. Then you made roasted beets and yams dribbled with pesto and wild rice with mushrooms and sprouted adzukis.

Then John Wayne was in the Union and took a southern woman hostage. Of course they fall in love but it's slow going and she keeps trying to get him killed. Maybe we think if we adopt a baby you won't die. Maybe we think we're too lucky or too decadent sitting over the highlands bluffs just us looking at seals who are logs. Coming, going, walking, writing, doing our little things, reading our big fat art books.

Music is everything. You put on Otis when I was in the bath and you were cooking, and that turned into something else. We stopped and listened to that Bright Eyes song. I said I'm glad I didn't die before I met you. You said, Swear I was born right in the doorway.

07.21.2014

Yesterday the sun came in through the shutters, big Ronald was crying on the floor. He likes to be invited into the bed. I invited him up, he leapt his 100-lb body up the four feet. In Japan making a pot of tea is an art: I took yesterday's grounds and yesterday's bag and boiled water and poured it in.

We sat at the table, yesterday, to do this typing. It was a weekend. We debated not doing it. What is the difference between our weekends and our weeks? We did it, typing at the table—battleship style—instead of the bed.

The project was already making me sad. There's so much to cover, and no time for reflection, or explanation. And because we are going to wait to show each other, it's like a secret, though it's just about what we've done. You won't talk about it much. And the constraint grows. I follow your lead (always) and don't talk about it much. It's bubbling along, like we're learning to play a new two-person instrument, or like we're the four legs in an animal costume, learning to walk.

We drove (I drove) to the town to cheat on our diet. I can still be bad, but with rules, and not every day. This will help relax me, and stop the spread of bad cells. Organic bagel with lox. You had the gluten-free scone. All were delicious. I had to promise not to regret it—that could cause inflammation. I didn't regret it, I don't. I had tea, you had decaf cappuccino. Your gluten-free scone was fantastic, but I knew there was too much sugar. Your cappuccino smelled like god, but how do they get the caffeine out? The Water Method. But how much water does that waste?

Behind us, two older women talking freely about male sexuality. One was the mentor, active in revolution. You told me I missed it when I was getting the drinks, the countries she's been to. I only remember Israel. But they were talking about one husband, his resentment at his wife for limiting his sex life to only her. Something else about intimacy vs. fun. Wild assumptions: all men are this way, can't imagine Donnie caring about sex but he must at least dream about it.

Yesterday we walked from there and saw one lady walking a little dog and one lady walking an alpaca. I told you I'm so glad I'm here. I said yesterday I saw an alpaca. Yesterday I saw an alpaca, I wanted to crawl inside its furry shell, to ride it into the ocean, to drink a toddy with its owner, who wore alpaca and looked like an alpaca and walked the monster on a leash. Its alpaca lips curled and it didn't seem to notice me, yesterday.

We walked the circumference of the city, overlooking the ocean. The headlands. Now that we live on the coast the ocean's an ambience. I remember how it used to make me cry to see it, but this postcard still feels portable, small, somehow. I tricked you into walking to this little trail where we could watch what I thought were otters but were seaweeds. Your poor knee condition. My poor cancer condition. You're not allowed to even have a malady anymore.

Yesterday we shopped for groceries, we went to a woodworking show, we saw a smithy shop. I love your poem "he works for a smithy." We saw the art market, craftspeople with their wares. I heard someone say, "Everyone speaks seven languages." I got defensive.

It's funny to organize a day this way, not weighing the things but just letting them go, chronologically. I looked at my iPad a lot. Day 1 Buffalo Bills training camp. My favorite player didn't pass his conditioning test. We ate. I gave you a massage. We did it. I made dinner. We watched a movie. You made popcorn. You fed the dogs. We watched another movie. We swore to stop watching movies on the vacation. We went to bed.

JULY 22, 2014

Yesterday was a long time ago.

You made an omelette with all we had.

I did one-legged jump backs into chataranga.

You did pull-ups in the kitchen door.

I took a deep bath.

And read the black soap bottle from Olympia, Washington, with fair trade in West Africa. Of course Olympia.

What is this a record of hippie haven.

We went to the *Snowpiercer*.

Pale imitation of Terry Gilliam or the more bright brutal apocalypses. All film is the train metaphor. How did that kid get a fur suit tailored exactly to his size for cuteness. What happened to her clairvoyance. How come they never get truly fucked up. Captain America's bottom lip is too big for the part. I didn't see his arm get churned off. Movie moves from back to front of the train, a movie in reverse. All the little cabins. Nice job.

Not raving about The Ravens, I said. View over the high treetops. Two different people on separate balconies off their rooms under the chimneys. One on her phone, one just looking. She is on her phone because one arm wrapped around her waist and the other holding her face. Someone else just looks out over the trees.

Piles of cedar firewood for the people in their rooms. We wait for a table and I stand in front of the fire with my back to it. Is it obvious I'm just trying to warm my ass. Is it that obvious.

Families unpacking from cars into the lodge. Trauma camping. One boy in athletic wear runs across the parking lot with a large clear plastic bag containing clothes. Did someone tell him to run or is this just his pleasure. Light a fire under it, son, where is your sense of urgency. No one will say that to this child.

I try to remember to tell about the birds—hawks, ravens, whatever—over the yoga deck. One comes so close I hear his wings clap over my head. What color was he, you ask. Black. From underneath.

But I don't want to be about the birds.

07.22.2014

Yesterday was nothing but gloom, the day never started, there was tea, many vegetables in an omelet from the tiny kitchen, the pan was too big, but I got the eggs to fold over. I guess we're ovo-vegan-something. I did my workout, had to cheat on the pull-ups a bit, but it burned and I felt strong.

There was so much gloom. It was fog and spray and shade on shade. Immediately you suggested a movie. I'm always up for that. But first we read. De Certeau. I revised a bio for *The Volta*.

We took the dogs to the beach, walked them in the gloom. K started screaming as soon as we got there, she was once one traumatized pooch. She screamed and we listened to her. It's an incredible sound. Poor thing.

I walked the dogs, as your knee was hurting and these wild animals can pull you apart. They sniffed like they were on the trail of something, 150 pounds of muscle and teeth. Ronald took a shit as soon as he walked 10 feet. I put the shit in a bag. There were a few people around. I carried the shit about 100 yards to a garbage can, kept getting twisted in their lines. I could see you contemplating eternity on the beach. I plopped the bag of shit into the garbage can. The dogs pulled me every which way. I didn't want to snap them too hard, too many people watching. We started walking towards you. K shat in some cover of sea plants. She walks around a bit when she does it. I had one more bag. You were walking closer, I thought if I gave you the two dogs for the moment, I could bag K's shit better. I walked towards you, 20 feet or so, R took a second huge shit. I handed you R's reigns. I only had one bag. I bagged R's shit. Carried its weight back to the can. Left K's shit to the rain.

Later, *Snowpiercer*. 95% fresh critically, 90% fresh audience. I have many thoughts about it. I felt the energy there, class & violence. The train as filmstrip, Tilda Swinton as the surreal visitor from the rich front. Captain America was poor and Jackson Pollock made him eat babies, they tasted the best, and the only way to destroy capitalism is to blow through the side with a stolen collection of drugs and roll down the mountain off the rails and look at a polar bear. I cannot disagree.

We had the most expensive vegan dinner of our lives. You were not that into it. We like my cooking better, but it's so hard to cook so well. We saved half of it for tomorrow, better known as today.

JULY 23, 2014

Yesterday we made a rash decision.

Ended up in a hotel room in Goleta watching sports in a king-size bed by a pool. Slept with the lights on until 4 then watched some more Sports Center and you walked to the Valero for water. Both dogs at the foot of the bed.

Before that I drove us into town, into the college part of town. College kids yelling and eating. All of a sudden running out of their dorms at 9:30 at night. That makes sense to me in a way I remember, although isolated. Two or three friends walk together. Blond girls in yoga pants with golden retrievers. Boys walk down alleys alone. No one is more alone than the males, which explains a lot of the problems everyone else has.

To get there I drove us in night through the hills and over the cliffs and couldn't see but I didn't want to tell you, wanted to do my half. You did the traffic and the highway and the forest. I opened the roof so we could all see the whole thing, all of us, the dogs. We ate a bit of leftovers from Ravens in the car, a mushroom crepe, some potato salad. I fed you mouths of black rice.

Before that we packed. I did my gathering routine and you did the carrying. How many times have we moved house. At the end, the dishes. I gathered all our empty jars, every bag, all the produce we just bought. Packed it all with cold packs. These are the things I can do. A bottle bag with vitamins and supplements.

I get a melanoma alert on my phone about a professor-astronaut who had Stage 3 and now has Stage 4 and is on a trial of the MK-3470. The same as going into space, he says, there is an individual component and a collective one. He says you'll do anything to stay alive. He and his wife are both astronauts, it says, they went up to space together in the '80s. Twice. They have two children. What are the odds.

On our way out of town in the morning, after packing up the rented house that's become claustrophobic and gray, we drive by a neighbor in his yard. He is standing over some part of garden with no expression. I wave and smile and hate myself, what is my mood, what message. He looks our age and possibly dreadlocked. He waves back somewhat glad or surprised or neither.

We forget to pull up directions on our phone and so drive around in a circle back to the house to poach the internet one last time. We drive by the neighbor's house again, I'm ready to be embarrassed or not wave a second time, but he's gone.

07.23.2014

Yesterday more gloom, we pay for this in California? We were both sad to have 5 more days. We have other places we could be. The privilege is astounding, but we could just roll. We are trying to vacate, and so we decided to vacate.

It went like this: we tried to make a breakfast of some sort, it was fine. We had tea. Supplements. We were looking at each other. I don't know who said we could go today or tomorrow. We had a new renter in our house and she couldn't work the coffee grounder, it said on your phone. You had an amazing solution—the magic bullet! We began to dislike the tactics our temporary landlord employed, basically no tactic at all but cellphone silence.

I called the hotel we would stay at near Santa Barbara, see if we could switch our reservation for on the way home. We could, but it would cost more, it would be for today. We hated the house we were in. We came here to see if we could write, and had proven that who knows, but maybe. We said let's go. I was on the phone. They had a room. All the reviews were terrible. You said you wanted to, were tired of being cold. Tired of staying in someone's home. I was tired of it too, of having cable, of the routine we'd grown, tired of the choices. Typing these things made me even more aware of it, how much time was downtime, which is what you do when you vacate, but I wanted to move. I thought of how many times the one radio station had played Counting Crows, how I always thought they were ridiculous, but how I kind of liked what they were up to in Mendocino. I accepted the reservation. It was noon or so and we had an eight-hour drive ahead. You gave me the nod.

You packed the stuff, I packed the car. I made an ingenious structure out of bungees that held the backseat dog hammock up while providing support for our various baggage. You packed so fast, I packed so fast, we were out of there in an hour.

Yesterday we drove from Albion, CA, to San Bernardino, CA. I drove five hours, you drove almost four. We ate leftovers and talked and listened to the radio and looked at our phones. I drove through redwoods and mountains and we marveled at the shade. We were free. We drove and drove. The news was about shot-down planes getting sawed in half by diesel saws and Tony Dungy being a bigot. I thought about *Snowpiercer*, about the rebels winning and owning the same system. Like I was supposed to.

Yesterday we ordered, obtained, and metabolized pizza, which we are not supposed to do. The website mentioned organic ingredients. We found our hotel. It was still under construction.

TWO

07.24.2014

Yesterday we woke in Goleta a few times. We had passed out from the driving fatigue, and we woke up twice. I was glad to see you had the TV on. We watched radio sports anchors talk into their microphones. Mike and Mike. One bigger than another. You noticed that one Mike in their logo was bolded. I walked the grounds looking for concessions, H_2O. Ended up at a nearby Sonoco, bought two bottles of water from a funny guy. Returned incredibly proud of myself. We went back to sleep, in an expensive hotel under construction.

We woke again, later—we had slept in! I took the dogs out to the tumult of the hotel they were building right around us. They were using diesel saws to cut the pavement in half. Workers everywhere, fumes and falling dust. $200. I worried about how we might come off in this project with our little bougie details. Ronald shat under the hedge. We returned. We watched a news channel we had never seen before, one where they talked about Nestlé bottling desert water in 20-minute interviews with brilliant women. It totally passed the Bechdel test. You and I walked to get acai bowls and to survey the renovation.

We ate our delicious superfood bowls. Prepared for a swim. Went to the pool. Saw the cloud of chemicals, the rusty light floating there. Changed our plans. Smelled acetate everywhere, got lightheaded, got high. Time to split.

Another detail: we weren't going to our real house, we were going to our other place: our land in Landers, the place we bought to get away. I drove.

You called Pappy's to get a table in two days, left a message. Some band is playing. Desert chic hipster super saloon. I drove through steadily browner mountains. You wrote an incredible letter to the hotel chain that is buying our renovated hotel. I could hear our money coming back to us. Teamwork.

I drove. You were on your phone — reading me the backlash many adopters felt when parenting interracially. You read me how we would have to train our family, ourselves. How difficult it was, has always been. How there are so many things you cannot say, how every word must be controlled so as not to hurt deeper than we could imagine. I listened to a '90s hero, Mac from Superchunk talk about his label, Merge's, 25th anniversary on the satellite radio. Thought of the scenes I grew up in, DIY mixed with all the badness of youth, but with politics. Would I hate me now?

Yesterday we rambled the artist's lives, without making any art. We stopped at a health food store in the middle of the desert. I ate an apple, drank coconut water, ate something called a coconut square, some kale chips. I thought a little about the tumor I had, about the cells in me that I could kill with the apple. You drove the last hour and a half. I looked at the Buffalo Bills training camp updates on my phone — the prized rookie had made an amazing one-handed catch that had gone viral. I looked out the window, thought about the desert, how all these enormous box stores had gotten here.

We got to our palace in Landers. It was wonderful. Hot. Ours. I carried everything in from the car, you put everything away. I twisted hammock hooks into two trees in the shade, moved our hammocks there. You hobbled out on your bum knee. We laid on hammocks in the shade in the heat. You said, Holy shit. You saw a coyote and sprang to chase it off. It was so cute. K went crazy. Tried to crawl under the fence. We let her have it, played fierce loving parent. She was good and sorry.

Yesterday I started to understand how to simultaneously make beans and rice in the same pressure cooker. It was good and clean. I did my martial arts video workout. You tried yoga, but your poor knee.

We read. You: some book about Jacques Tati. Me: *Text for Nothing/On Certainty*. A cricket chirped everywhere, amplified, and we couldn't find it.

JULY 24, 2014

Yesterday: two large rocks painted white. Stacked on top of each other on the side of the desert road. Spray painted in blue scrawl: TUBS.

A pile of trash on Happy Trail. Open dark plastic trash bag and signs of human. Plastic wrapping for toilet paper. Plastics.

A woman and her teenage daughter in line at BJs Health Foods. Her man comes up behind her, begins patting her on her waist and hips. Large hips. He keeps patting almost like a child, or like dough. Patting and patting.

He runs to get something at the other end of the store. The girl in Spanish tells him to hurry, I think, motions him impatient. He runs back just in time, playful, gets his item in for checkout. Pats his lady on the hips. Then he moves around and pokes the girl in her back where her bra strap would be. She recoils in a sharp move, scolds him, not having it.

We drive from where the green turns into all blue sea and empty yellow beaches. I remember we saw a dead seal there years ago. Ronald Johnson found it, sniffed it. That was before Kiki Smith, on our trip to Chicu & Suzanne's wedding when our car was broken into and everything got stolen because we didn't use the valet at the fancy hotel in the big city San Francisco. We never made it to the wedding. Instead I think we drove all night and broke down in Iowa with a clutch. Your dad saved us with money.

Then the beaches turn into rock hills and desert when I look up again.

You drive, I research transracial adoption. It's a problem, mainly because white people and Christianity and privilege. You can't shut the child down, you will never understand, negative capability. Whatever you do will not be enough, it's important to note.

I drive us from Hesperia to Landers, we are so glad to be here, not in the gray rented house but in our own modern cabin with stained green concrete floors, modern blue sectional couch, plywood table on saw horses. Orange mod molded chairs. The view of the hills we are inside a western.

You move the hammocks from under the deck to under the trees. It's been too long since we've been inside a hammock, more than a week.

I see a coyote out of the side of my eyes and for some reason I jump up and run over to him. We look at each other, me and the coyote, who is the size of Kiki Smith but brown. With a more Waspy face, fine upturned nose and slendernesses. We look in each other's eyes. I shoo him off and feel bad about it, some maternal disease. Kiki Smith tries to crawl out to find him. Ronald Johnson doesn't notice or doesn't care.

You move the hammocks back under the deck when the shade comes. The sun is already down and the sky is turning orange on all sides. The show starts. It cools down and a breeze. Ronald and Kiki come running from the end of the land. They are running so fast I don't know how they'll stop but they do. They drink water. We all play fetch.

My knee is terrible now, I can't even do yoga. You box in the bedroom and make rice & beans in the pressure cooker, together, spicy. We eat in front of a view. Boulder hills and many shades of brown expanse and sky.

We turn on the dog's lights and let them run. Kiki goes all the way to the back, so far away you have to go corral her. We don't look at the stars for long. I finish a book on Jacques Tati. You bring me a cold pack in a towel. I wake up a few times hallucinating bugs or feeling them.

When we got here there was a very large camel spider in the kitchen sink in the drain on his back. Clear white with articulated joints and digits, scalpel pincers. We smashed him but we let the cricket crick under our bed all night.

07.25.2014

Yesterday was a desert day, a day spent acknowledging your knee and its troubles. I woke up, let the dogs out to run this five-acre fenced plot of ours, made some tea. This place is home now, one of our homes, and I can feel the peace on a cellular level. No internet. No TV. Just distances and a house to work on.

I made the best smoothie ever. I have the recipe down now. It involves a lot of raw organic cacao powder, which is somehow healing. I slathered myself in sesame oil to keep from burning out there. We drank our smoothies out back and typed about yesterday. The sun was coming over the house, making the table I was typing on brighter and hotter, encroaching on my laptop. I moved it onto my knee. You saw that and let me have it a bit, which I deserved, about the toxic fields around these machines, the poisons they are made of, how since you've known me I've always had a device of some kind touching my body, how the cancer must be from my intimacy with Apple products. You're right. I thought of how I'd lie back on the couch with my iPad so often, digging it into my flesh as a kind of stand, how the bad cells must love that, how it must inflame the area even now.

Yesterday I changed a bunch of interior doorknobs around. We have an interesting arrangement of doorknobs, and I consulted with you to determine where to put them. We have four interior doors: one for the bathroom, one for the closet, and two for the bedrooms. The closet and bedrooms are all off the same hallway, therefore they can all be included in one eyeshot. We have purchased: one silver lever doorknob without a lock, one with a lock, and one darker-hued levered knob (which I bought on overstock.com, thinking it was two sets of knobs, as it was labeled). We prefer levered knobs in this house because they enhance the gallery aesthetic. You helped with the solution, which I am vaguely happy with. Locking lever on the closet. Silver non-locking on the bedroom, darker non-locking on the other bedroom (which is often in some shade), and locking standard knob from one of the bedrooms on the bathroom, should we ever have guests the lock will come in handy. I'd like to get a locking lever sometime. You prone on the couch icing your knee.

I made some leftover lunch and it was fine.

What else happened yesterday? A lot of commerce. We went to the used appliance store. We debated many of our needs. We found the perfect refrigerator, a combo washing machine/dryer, and an amazing vintage kitchen stove. I'm ashamed how excited I am by these things. The men at the place were so nice, they fix them up theirselves, showed us the special stock, and gave us great deals and water. We tried to speak a little Spanish with them. They will be delivered on Monday, because we have to wait for a part for the fridge.

We went looking at thrift stores in Joshua Tree/Yucca Valley for lamps. We got two pairs of boots for you, three records (Leonard Cohen, Genesis, The Kinks), a set of bowls that you loved, and a splendid typewriter. Then we went (more shame) to Walmart, the museum of America, and suffered. You hobbled all around there. We bought a vacuum, some clothespins, I can't remember what else. Some knee braces. I was almost run over by an able-bodied man in a scooter with a chicken in his basket. I could go on about Walmart, but I hope never to have to. We swore we'd never come back.

We made it back, hammocked for awhile, had a handful of nuts. Watched the sun go down, and watched a little after, which is better. K picked up a limp along the way.

I learned how to make vegan macaroni and cheese. Quinoa shells and cashew cheese. When I set it in to bake in your new bowl, I did an impossible leg workout. I fell over a hundred times.

You were hungry and so was I and we ate our dinner. I also learned that if you soak limp lettuce in an icebath, it revives the crunch.

I learned a lot yesterday. I made a tiny fire in the chimenea. We puffed on the Panda. Watched a Marlon Brando western on the laptop. *The Appaloosa*. You couldn't buy it. I was all in. It was super meta, and Brando is the weakest western hero you could find, until the end when you see he can overcome a scorpion sting and that he has a little talent for killing.

JULY 25, 2014

Yesterday I was going to write all about you.

You made the bancha tea in the morning, then cacao-blueberry smoothies.
You changed all the doorknobs and made them levers and made the closet
lock. You made rice and adzukis with a head of kale. You brought out the
flavor tray. You made us a chilled water with ice and lemon before driving
into town, but then you left it in the fridge.

You drove us into town for appliances and a box store. You carried the gift
cards from your sister two years ago Festivus. You checked on the Buffalo
Bills on your phone and tuned in to the NFL channel on the radio.

You showed me where the sporting goods were so I could find a knee brace
while you looked for an onion in the impossible Andy Warhol shopping
place. You noticed the obese couple in matching scooters.

You loaded the bowl and noticed how good I am at smoking. You made
gluten-free vegan mac and cheese like it was not a thing. You queued up
the Marlon Brando film, the Western where he tries a Mexican accent with
blue eyes and a disgusting mop of blond hair, fake beard. You noticed the
glue on the beard.

You played guitar lying on your back on the blue couch. You worked out
hard.

We bought used appliances from Carlos. A Samsung fridge he was working on in the back, only showed us later. A washer-dryer that does it all, even thought we've had one before, it was Italian and broke and we couldn't afford the repair. For some reason we think this one will be better, it's an LG. A stove we only see on the way out, white frosted glass from the '80s. Carlos likes the old things like we do. He gives us bottles of water, is a gentleman from some other time. You're worried we won't be able to get all that money out of the credit union, but there it is.

We go to the Picking Shack and get a typewriter, Underwood. I get two pairs of boots, one calf tan with fringe mid-rise, another low-rise black suede with silver buttons. Dingo and Minnetonka. Cheap. I don't even really think about it, thrift store shoes, I don't even wonder if they'll be stinky, they look so new. Even the bottoms have no wear.

Right away you see a reel-to-reel you want, the guy says it comes with tapes, Who knows it could be Kennedy and Marilyn. You don't buy it. I find a set of four nesting Pyrex serving bowls for so little, burnt orange color with a white harvest print. We get a Leonard Cohen record, a Kinks one with everything, and the good Genesis.

We buy a vacuum at the box store. I remember all the vacuums we've had that don't work and how we could have afforded the good one by now.

Yesterday I really couldn't walk finally and went into public with my limp. I like limping, I know that's terrible. I like the way I am a problem, people can finally see my problems with a limp. But I'm probably wrong, people probably don't think, Oh that poor girl with the limp, like I'm in 5th grade or something. They probably think, Woah, that's a fucked- up woman with a limp.

Walking the entire width of the box store to where you pointed is the most difficult, I almost don't make it. I walk there to get a knee brace. I get two. I move so slowly I see everything.

The obese man in the scooter grabs a full chicken from the rotisserie first thing. I tell you about that later. How is he going to shop with that chicken in his cart, won't it spoil.

At home we try to walk barefoot on the sand to get grounded. I think you're barefoot so I go barefoot. I get burned and you have flippers on I see.

Kiki comes up limping in the evening. I think she's in sympathy with me. There's no thorn and no cut but she licks and licks her left front paw. We have some confusion about what is a dog's right and what is a dog's left when I try to tell you which one. I can't see what's wrong with the paw, there is no outward sign.

I fall asleep before the movie's over. I don't smoke enough. The typewriter looks supreme on the faux-denza you made. I read lots of Anne Waldman, I look at all the pictures. I'm glad someone is talking about these things.

I wonder what you write about in here.

07.26.2014

Yesterday had clouds from the beginning, even a little rain here and there, desert weirdness, stunning: sun over clouds and breezes. It kept the heat down below 100 and we kept the windows open all day. It was a peaceful day: never into town until evening, books and a few projects, lots of staring into the sun. I don't feel like I did anything. I slept a lot, hung in a hammock and stared at the horizon.

The days when you can't remember much might be the best days. We shouldn't have brought the phones inside. I checked them a few times. Nothing to see there. Nothing in the world.

We were in the world enjoying our place at Kickapoo trail. I exercised early, legs on fire, squats and crazy jumps from my DVDs. I felt competent in my body, some strength growing there but shameful balance and flexibility. Soaked in sweat, looked at my scar in the mirror before showering.

You had a good day too. You wrote. You read. We tried to inhabit different rooms a bit, see if we can get some habits, sequester ourselves in our own creative spaces. I wrote a bit of a poem in bed, no idea how to do it, something with Wittgensteinian logic and Beckett ambivalence, but my own pathetic version. I cannot understand how a poem can be good, how it can consider an audience, no wonder it comes down to accessibility, personality, coterie, and Facebook campaigns.

Smoothie for breakfast, you cooked some deliciousness from scraps we had lying around in the fridge for lunch. We were going to Pappy's for dinner later, so we ate light. I forgot, when I woke up I made my first batch of cashew milk. Here's a recipe: soak one cup of cashews in water overnight. In the morning, rinse the cashews and place them in the blender with 3 cups of water, part of a date, and maybe some vanilla. Blend 'til milk. I filtered mine with a fine strainer, but they have nut milk bags too. I shall try this with hemp seeds soon.

The dogs had a good day. We had one too. I'm sure I'm leaving so much out, yes I am, the way I took down a desk anchored to the wall to go with the chair I cannot get casters on, how I don't have any wall anchors and will have to get them today. What a change it makes having my clothes in another room, how much neater it is to have yours in our bedroom. How we vacuumed with our new vacuum, not for cleanliness, but to see if it would work.

Dinnertime we went to Pappy and Harriet's Pioneertown Palace for dinner and entertainment. Dinner was good, we shared a half organic chicken. I have my issues about this, being vegan every other way, except for occasional eggs, but it is more about filling in missing nutrition than ethics at this point. And this chicken was healthy before we ate it and it was raised nearby. I had my seldom-applied glass of red wine. I thought about the antioxidants, the B-12 this dinner offered. The kale salad was different tonight, there was baby kale in there.

I would like to describe Pappy's to the uninitiated reader, but sometime later. The band was terrible in the most memorable way. That dance the singer did. I bet you covered that. We left fairly early.

Panda and stars and a great conversation about Brando vs. Newman, about being a savior at 25, how could one recover from that? Start a somewhat ethical food company. Learn to act. We watched *Jeremiah Johnson* and it was ok, but not the movie I thought it was going to be, which is what I go to the movies for.

JULY 26, 2014

Yesterday I tried to remember little things for today. I watched an animal for a long time to see if it hopped.

Yesterday it rained in the desert. Sideways rain through the screens. All the smells changed and molted.

You stayed in the hammock a long time in the wind. I hobbled over but went back inside. You climbed the stairs I couldn't climb to the roof with the dogs.

I learned Spanish. *Amarillo* and *blanco*, *comer* and *corre*. I am a child inside any language.

I made brown rice mixed with wild rice and yams. We ate outside facing the back after the rain. You wiped off the table, which had brown dots. Either dirty rain or dirty table.

I read too much Anne Waldman. A little David Byrne, a little Wittgenstein. Fourteen things from Thích Nhất Hạnh. Where is Vietnam Buddhism in Anne Waldman. She goes to Nicaragua, she goes to India, she goes to Nam. It sounds like maybe she smokes an opium pipe and fucks young girls there. But I can't prove it in language.

David Byrne is a thief. But, he says, he thinks that's ok. Now I remember why I stopped reading that book.

I look forward to Pappy's all day. We see some brother band from "the Midwest." Where is the Midwest, bring it to me. On second thought, keep it.

We laugh at the ridiculous dance moves the singer has. Side to side heel slide in women's Levis jeans. I say women don't wear women's Levi's jeans. All of his songs are about women, not like The Kinks. He wears his long light brown hair in a loose gel curl. I'd like to see the look on David Byrne's face.

We almost argue when you don't notice the misogynist lyrics. Then you do. I like the way men look at you, I like it when they get you in the back seat of their car. He is the only one with a wedding ring, I notice. I say, how can she abide, you say, there's no accounting for taste.

We laugh when I sing, You Say Yes, I Say No, operatic, sort of to myself. Maybe I'm trying to be funny and maybe I'm just singing a little Beatles tune. Maybe I wasn't thinking about it, which makes me laugh harder, wipe tears into my face cream.

We sit out back in the way back chairs and look up. I see one star move inexplicably and a cloud of white dust spread out. You say aliens are rocks. I believe it too.

07.27.2014

Yesterday I decided paragraphs need not be employed here. These demarcations of what? some secondary kind of presence. These are not dramatic days, they need not be organized by some method, some kind of heterodoxy thing. I didn't read much, but I read closely. I woke up too early, K had to go outside, or wanted to, and I walked out there in my underpants. I don't wear many bikini briefs, but this is the second home, where I keep my backups. Each of my other backups bear a hole in the butt, right where my asshole is. Somehow it bothered you when I would wear them at home, so I wore these out into the desert, where K had gone too far. Such a pleasure, to know no one will see you, or care, in your red bikini briefs with a hole in the ass. I made tea and Irish oatmeal with chia and hemp seeds in the pressure cooker. Dumped a million healthy things on it. Drowning melanoma with the superstuffs. Bee pollen isn't vegan. It was always too early, desert time, time to go to town to the farmer's market so we can get the big bag of exotic mushrooms. It's a 30-minute drive, but everyone says it takes 10. Was it hot? It's the desert, nothing is left over, even the sand is an example. We have a poster in our bathroom at home, Norma Cole assemblage, and it says that last line last and it's by my friend and colleague Michael Davidson, poet, cooker of rabbit, and scholar of modern and contemporary poetry. You looked very beautiful, but still hobbled. I drove, I checked our post office box (3138?—still learning the #) and we received: junk mail, a *Mother Earth News*, and a plug for the laptop I got from my Sony scholarship two years ago. We went to town, to find some lamps, we didn't find any (a little mishap when I wanted to look more but you kept us on schedule and I was putting out some victim vibe), to see if the washing machine we bought was the one we really wanted (it was), to the bookstore to see what was up, it was a crazy place but there were lots of Beats for sure. Not necessarily in that order. We drove towards the mushrooms but first a quick stop at Home Depot for wall brackets, you stayed in the car but texted me about something for my swag light switcheroo and I checked for the cover I needed but they only had the one I already had, I'll modify it, I said to myself. Found the wall anchors, out of there in record time, too bad I needed some other things for my swag light switcheroo namely a switch that would match the other two switches I'd upgraded on that part of the wall. We drove to the farmer's market and refreshed our veggie stock, I'm glad you wanted to go there last on our excursion, very logical, that way the veggies didn't wilt in the hot car. We went to the natural food store and bought more healthy things. Somewhere around here I said you can drive if you want, I was a little off all day yesterday and I'm sorry your knee should not be pressing the throttle down or the gas pedal and I wouldn't let you drive when you said you wanted to because you didn't want to drive, I wanted to drive, but I wanted it acknowledged that I was driving. I drove us home and we listened to the radio I cannot remember what we heard. Later I programmed the B bank on our Sirius XM radio so we could have more stations at our fingertips. There is a special one where Tom Petty has taken over everything and I like Tom Petty fine, more as a man than as a songwriter though I like his early stuff and his late stuff, just not really the middle stuff, but he was being interviewed on this station in a public forum and someone asked him about his guilty pleasure and he didn't have one because Tom Petty has no guilt. But here's something you may not know about me, he said, I was recently made a bachelor again and I wanted a normal life, not to you know marry a stripper or something so I got really into the NBA and now I schedule our tours around the playoffs. I fixed a bunch of things later in the day and napped a bunch, moved the desk down the wall with my new anchors, changed the swag lamp into a switched lamp (I used an old switch that doesn't match, but that part's easy to change later), I fixed *My Life in CIA* by finishing it (I dunno about Harry Mathews, but the end was crazy enough), read something about Method and Modern American Poetry, slept a bunch, turned the A/C on and off, watched you writing and reading and learning Spanish, took the dogs out, made dinner (quinoa pasta and crazy mushrooms), started reading Bernadette Mayer's *Hunger Notebooks* or whatever it's called, did yoga with sports radio on, and had that conversation with you about how hard it is to write after cancer. Frankly, Adorno, it's barbaric.

JULY 27, 2014

Yesterday I couldn't even imagine your prose. What does it mean when you say you're writing prose? I can't conceive a non-reflexive, de-sonorized literary you.

Yesterday I read little Ben & Feliz & Brett's *The Wes Letters* in entirety. I was impressed with how specifically life happened in front of them, inside them. They seemed at once high school and fractured catapulted adult. They never seemed out of time.

I wrote in a large soft pink notebook on a green table that you lowered to meet the steel-cased orange chair. I wrote with a black pen with a black rubber finger guard. Ribbed, it rubbed. I hated my handwriting. One thing about page writing is that I'm less tempted to go back and read it, so that's something, maybe something good. I don't like to re-read.

Yesterday we laid around on the blue couch a lot. Under the windows with views of mountain desert rocks brush and sand. Lots of sky.

We went to the farmer's market in Joshua Tree in a parking lot and made a beeline for the mushroom man. We got the large medley basket for $13.00. We still have a jar of reishis we should grind up into powder. We stopped at every vegetable booth and got two heirloom tomatoes, a peach, a nectarine, some black kale, a round green zucchini, one basket of strawberries, one basket of blackberries, one red onion, one white onion, a head of basil. A yellow squash I've never seen before, splatted with green almost action-painted. Eleven okra.

Two small boys walked a very small dog and I wrote about that elsewhere. We talked about writing, this trauma, writing post-cancer, how everything is so serious now it's hard to be funny or want to. It's hard not to talk about it, but neither of us wants to talk about it.

We planned a documentary of my father about the sex changes. We'll record interviews with him and interviews with my brother the yogi. Male body, feminine occupation, deviation, détournement. We talked about how he won't talk to me about it, which has become the major feature of this story. I can't get the story. I told you I might include you, the third male, health and the body and healing. But maybe that's another thing. You'll write the music and I'll write the soundtrack.

In the evening, you cooked pasta and the mushrooms. In the day, I made okra and polenta. I burned some onions in there and we had to pick them out. I don't know what to do with okra, you said. I said, I do. Oklahoma food. Cook them until they don't slime.

We read and read and read. So much the dogs hardly played.

I thought about all the furniture we made: the plywood table on saw horses, the faux credenza out of cabinets, the coffee table out of concrete pylons and glass, the bookshelves, the cinder block and post bed and bench. At evening we sat out back at the table we made out of a door and concrete and ate and looked at the sky.

We played cribbage. You won.

Out back there were two bats who at first looked like small birds. They flew so close and fast I could see the points on their wings. I told you about how when I was a nanny in Italy and would finally get off the job, I would go swimming at dusk, and the bats would dive at me in the pool picking up bugs off the surface.

We went inside. We didn't smoke.

07.28.2014

Yesterday all day in the desert, I woke and looked at some books. Looked at *Mother Earth News*. I remember looking at my parent's copies when I was a kid, but they were hippies. This is some kind of off-the-grid low-content survivalist shit. The liberals flee the sticks, back to the cities. The militia reclaims the hills. Rupert Murdoch buys a hundred magazines with a twitch of his finger. They pay the writers nothing, so they can't write. I don't know, it's a theory. What happened to good people on the land? Off grid because oil is shit. I read words in books, not books. There was an ad for a composting toilet with a proud woman poised next to it, I had to show it to you, I think I woke you with it. I would be proud to compost my own shit: it's on the list. Solar wind power with a garden and a dehydrator. Much of yesterday we looked for used hot tubs on Craigslist on our one-bar phones. We had a smoothie for breakfast, I think you made it, very good, grapefruity, very good. I forgot that I woke up early and did a workout under the observation deck, like at 7:30, some upper-body thing where you let yourself down slowly for a three count then spring up quickly. That's one rep. I don't have the gear for the chin-ups so I used my TRX straps instead. There were clouds all day, even a little sprinkle but I did not know this would be the way and tried to beat the heat and it worked. I think it's called isometric motion. My little muscles rang out. I sweat like I always do. I could tell you woke up because I saw R investigating the premises. Usually K wakes me up, under the premise that she has to pee, I remember now she did, then the magazines (but I didn't show you the ad then, it was later or earlier), then the workout, you slept in a little bit. I came back in, we did our things, drank our superfoods. I can feel myself changing cellularly.

I used the satellite radio to listen to the Sunday morning shows on C-SPAN. I did not know I had this capacity. The old guy from one of the networks asked Madeleine Albright if this was the worst the world has ever been, Israel/Palestine, Russia, and we pulled our ambassadors out of Syria. Not to mention our own border, sending all the kids back to be murdered in Honduras, in Guatemala. Madeline said we always just used to focus on Russia, so we didn't notice the rest of the world falling apart. I think we took a nap. Fox Morning came on starring the first interview with a new Tea Partier representative and the nap ended to turn it off. Chris Wallace, is that his name? Mike's son? I didn't feel creative at all, decided to learn some Spanish with Rosetta Stone. I thought I was further ahead. I want to catch up to you, to speak in Spanish about who is eating and who is cooking. The program is fun. I did a bunch of it. Am I learning? I want to continue. It's a good way to feel like you're on the internet when you're not. We were outside a lot, walking on the hot sand, getting grounded, that's the new thing. Cancer cannot live in an alkaline environment. I made some crazy version of chana masala for lunch, not bad, and later cauliflower steaks with tofu steaks with sundried tomato caper relish and tomato garlic coulis and asparagus. That was a good meal, I emailed it to Brett because we are supposed to be sharing recipes. I did some routine labor at some point, must have. Thought about starting my tenure file, did no such thing. We looked at our phones a bit too much. I did the dishes while you did Pilates in the other room, listened to the old-school college rock station, 10 years or older equals old, but it was good, we compared PJ Harvey to Beyonce, had some great conversations about our work, I really think you should add the new stuff to the old stuff for your Les Figues book, later we got stoned and this time I made sure you were getting decent hits, though I got a little paranoid and you counseled me and I researched which of the Spaghetti Westerns we had in our DVD box set were decent and my phone said that Quentin liked this one we had with Lee Van Cleef, *Death Rides a Horse*, and it was a very good recommendation, though I almost turned it off in the rape scene but I'm glad I didn't because fifteen years later those fuckers got what was coming to them.

JULY 28, 2014

Yesterday Amit's birthday. It's been over five years—Bowie—since we've seen him. My phone phobia kicked in around then, we lived in Denver. I've hardly talked to anyone since.

Yesterday I don't remember. Late wake up. Reading in bed until not reading in bed. Mountainous view.

Talking long in hammocks about names. Thurman is a good one. Don't you want to give a child at least one neutral name in case they switch genders. That might have been today.

On the bench out front in the early night. Faded blue metal spray painted bench not from this decade, or the last, or the last, or the last, or the last.

There are a lot of things I'm not saying. That goes without saying. I like that saying. Because even as it goes without saying, you're saying.

Lee Van Cleef was nicknamed "grandfather" by the young gun. They follow each other to kill the killers. Some of the shots are quite incredible, large faces fill a screen, a gun holstered at an angle.

It all starts with two rapes, one of a young girl, one of a mother. The young boy watches and later revenges. It's a rape fantasy *and* a revenge fantasy.

I write and I think the NFL comes in. We learn our Spanish. I hear you in the other room shouting at the computer who can't hear you. Until it hears you.

You type a lot longer now. I have no idea what your yesterdays are like.

I make five new pages. You make food that oughta be in pictures. The cauliflower steak and the tofu steak with the red pepper and tomato and caper sauce spread underneath like paint. Tiny asparaguses on the side. You send the recipe to Zehner.

I think I showered and washed my hair yesterday. When I opened the shower curtain to get out, Ronald & Kiki were both sitting right there waiting for me on the orange bath mat.

Kiki and Ronald both limp at different times. Ronald licks and licks his front left (or right) paw. But I can't find anything the matter.

We don't go anywhere. I finally get what I want out of Anne Waldman, the stories about her and Allen, her "spiritual husband." I tell you a little bit about it. You read Harry Mathews and Bernadette.

You worry that I'll be mad if the Harry Mathews is misogynist, which it is. I say it depends on if he's straight or not, which is true in a way and not in another. I can hear your breathing change and I see what it's like to worry for you. I don't want you to worry, so I say it's ok. I really don't want you to worry.

Is this abstract? I can't tell what abstract is anymore. I worry about this.

I go to bed worrying about the five-year lifespan, your five years left. I worry to the point where I remember that even if I worry it won't change the outcome and won't make it better if it comes true. I remember that if I worry too much, the relief that should be relief never really comes. Then I worry a little less. Then in the middle of the night I wake up with a feeling that you're going to be ok. More than five years ok.

Planning is the most radical thing.

07.29.2014

Yesterday we wanted to drive home but we had to wait for our appliances to be delivered. I kind of wanted to stay in the desert, it was a good place to be, didn't want to drive in the evening, but we missed our house in San Diego and it wasn't 100 degrees there. We waited for the call from Carlos' Appliance. Cooked whatever we had left, two meals, tofu with vegetables for breakfast (scramble) and didn't cook, rather blended all loose veggies in a smoothie. Poked around on Rosetta Stone, passed a few more levels, thought about the game they're playing there. I'm good at tests, but never learn anything. Playing elimination, watching the pictures come up. I learned "son," how to use it in a sentence. Did my crazy workout, MMX, crazy hits and punches—you joined in, your knee is feeling better. You were doing this one-legged version, very impressive. Haven't weighed myself in forever, but feel alright. Gotta get all the fat off, finally not for vanity, but for life. Cancer grows where the body is cold, fat is cold cold, the tumor grew on the fattest part of my body. We were in a holding pattern, waiting for a call so we could leave. We took a nap. We cleaned the house out, nice to return to a clean desert house. I heard the bugs crunch as I ran over them on the vacuum. I kept looking at the front of my phone to see if I'd missed the call, I kept turning the phone up. But I think the switch on the side, the silence switch, was switched, it always is. You told me, Make sure your phone isn't on silent. I thought it wasn't. The call came an hour before we learned it had come. I called them back. The part they'd ordered hadn't come. Can you deliver it in a week? I asked, of course, how bout ten days? Sure. Great. We'll get our things when we go back to our clean cabin in the desert with nice used appliances. You were ready to go, had really packed everything. I just did the tetris putting the bags in the car. Turned off the breaker that pumps water to the house, the hot-water heater. We had to carry our trash and recycling out, it barely fit in the back. The dogs were stoked to jump in the back of the oven car. You opened the gate. We rumbled down dirty Kickapoo Trail. Found our favorite dumpster behind Kelly's Future to dump our trash. One bag. Probably illegal, but how much illegal? I was sleepy already, you got tea for us at Ma Rouge. I sat in the car with the dogs, stared at my phone. We did the three-hour drive, non-stop this time. Listened to the news, to some flashes of music. This car we have, I can scroll through the stations with my thumb. It brings me anxiety but also confidence, DJ-ing like this, can't let a second go by with a lame song or a commercial. This is how we destroy the system. The dogs slept, they'd had so much freedom to roam and run at the land. You read me your phone updates about melanoma. I saw two cop cars in good hiding spots. I've really slowed my average speed since my diagnosis, I really check my blind spots now. I wondered how the house would look, wasn't there a wedding there, or a wedding party, who knows what happens there when strangers occupy your home. The garbage knows. You researched eating possibilities and vegan dog lifespans. We ordered Rancho's. I pulled off the 163, we opened the windows and felt the cool air, the ocean nearby. The dogs stood up. You picked up your birth control at CVS. I ran into Rancho's, grabbed our food (it was waiting a bit). It tasted good, but there was too much of it. I could see our garbage was full in the driveway, nowhere to put the recycling in the trunk. Trash in the recycling, recycling in the trash. All the world revolves around recycling. Flower stems and food chunks. But the house was clean enough, and we cleaned it more then were too tired for a movie. I started reading *The Berlin Stories*, took my melatonin and aspirin, and crossed over.

JULY 29, 2014

Yesterday.

I think you might be writing our days in chronological order, getting every
little thing. I don't think that's what I'm doing.

Our new used fridge was supposed to come, so I took things off the old one.
CA's poem "I Hope I'm Loud When I'm Dead." Every time it's better. It
sort of achieves the max of what everyone's been going for since the '50s.
From Frank O'Hara to Facebook. Nicely done, CA, I say.

Our new used fridge didn't come. Neither our new used washer-dryer nor
our new used white glass oven-stove.

We waited for appliances by sleeping, punching, and reading.

You made a soup I named galangalang. We wanted different flavors, and
noodles. Kelp noodles, which are next to nothing, next to the shirataki
noodles made out of the inner insides of some sort of yam. You say.

Maybe my yesterdays are too styled. How can I just report.

Kiki was desperate inside in the A/C. She is an animal who just wants to be
hot. Ronald just wants to be near me and it's probably wrong that I like that.

We wanted to hear sports and news. Colin Cowherd. I like arguing with

Colin. It's Colin! Like he's a friend or something. Why does Colin make so much money? He doesn't want to take the day off.

I could really fill in for Colin. He doesn't want to wear a Swaggy P jersey on his show, not because he doesn't want a Swaggy P jersey, but because, I know, he doesn't want to wear something as unflattering as a jersey. Polyester. Baggy. It would mess with his tight little look. I know this although he doesn't say it.

Colin doesn't like to shake hands, Colin prefers the fist bump. For bacteria. I want to tell Colin about all those hotel rooms he stays in. I think about this as I'm cleaning up our city house yesterday night after two weeks of renters. There is no way I can get rid of all the people germs on the doorknobs, the soap dispenser, the faucets, the refrigerator handle. All those surfaces, not to mention the beds. And I'm cleaning for myself, Colin, what do you think happens at those hotels? They don't give a shit about you, you're sleeping in cess.

I remember yesterday the term "genetic cesspool," which is at least one reason not to procreate. You say we'd be lucky to get away with a six-toed child. Remember we're probably related somehow. But I only remember this now, I didn't remember this yesterday.

I sleep while you learn Spanish, try to catch me.

Colin turns the phrase "violence against women" into "violence against people" and then goes on a fairly respectable liberal rant. This right here is why Colin Cowherd is paid so much. He will only go so far. He won't totally alienate the lady hitters. He's everyone-out-there's skinny geeky liberal friend with lots of money.

Colin repeats himself. Colin gets ripped off. Colin has another show in the afternoon. Colin is performance art, on video while on radio. Colin has big gums and little lips. Colin abstractly doesn't like it when other stations "treat women badly." Colin admits his attraction to men. Big deal.

Colin, all you're doing is reinscribing the power of your position and the hotness of mine. Why are you even talking to the Lakers? No one cares about the Lakers anymore. It's all about Cleveland, the Thunder, the Rockets, LeBron. The Clippers are the only LA team now. You just give me so much material.

I stand in the kitchen talking back to Colin. We pack up the desert house.

You drive us all the way home and I Yelp. We go back to where it seems green.

It rains in the desert. You say it's a hot rain, straight down. It's hot raining. I watch the drops on the concrete, fat, until they're not separate drops anymore but just one large wet spot.

Lily texts me to see if she can stay over for Ben & Feliz's wedding. Of course. Carmen texts me to see if we're in town. I wonder if they collaborated from Las Cruces.

I am trying to be better. I am trying to see people.

We eat Rancho's on our outside table in our yard. We don't see the neighbor who hates our guests and tells us in detail. I let Kiki bark to annoy her. We stop by CVS to get my birth control pills for free. I try to act like a normal person in public.

On NPR they are talking about norm core with Thomas Frank. I think he's the one who says, "I used to be a punk rocker." I imitate him for you because you miss this precious moment. We don't watch a movie or anything.

You unmake and remake the bed while I clean and put away. We sleep with the windows open and the fan on in the perfect weather in our house.

07.30.2014

Yesterday we slept in, until almost 10:30. I woke up at 6, went back to sleep. Our round bed had everything. The rest of the day was almost gone. I checked my school email, there was an oldie from last week that would have great impact on the rest of my life. The office at UCSD needed my materials for my tenure packet—some famous poet would write a letter of support but needed it by the end of the week. I had already put my tenure file off for a month because I thought I was going to die. I told you and we decided we'd drive it in today. Lots of emails, I didn't know what went in my packet. New book, and lots of old books for their shelves. We picked up some more. I was getting the books together in the studio and you brought me the wedding cake you'd found in the fridge. Remember how our leftover wedding cake was soaked in melted ice when we got home in the van, what 10 years ago? I am not supposed to have sugar. Rule #1. But it tasted like everything. Great white cake. You were into it. I guess you got so into it that you decided to juice fast the entire day. I wasn't prepared for that, longed to do some eating or cooking but ok. Lots of water. The day just kept passing by. I tried to make my CV look ok, and borrowed yours to copy all the things we've done together. All those readings, the Doller road show. You have the most beautiful CV. I copied it out in the studio, which got hotter and hotter. I took off my shirt. I like the way you use columns, and your formatting and attention to detail is top-notch. I showed you my CV, and you laughed and had me send it to you so you could make it ok. I rely on you for everything. You have everything, how can you prop me up for so long? And now, me, sick and sad. You write 40 pages while I write 4. It took me all day, what else happened? We drove to La Jolla, you passenged and I drivened. I dropped off my stuff, learned what else I needed. No one seemed to recognize me with my beard, especially Jody, who told me a few minutes later, and I realized I probably look insane. Thinner, huge beard, floppy sun hat. We drove towards the juice bar in Solana Beach, but on the way we stopped to get the dogs vegan dog food at Dexter's Deli (you had researched, and the V-dog website said they stocked it there). We saw that Bull Taco had opened a Bull Taco, which is supposedly organic. Dexter's had a sign that said they didn't support vegan dog food, but you found a dog in England who lived for 30 years on that diet. Imagine meat, imagine the meat Americans eat, imagine the meat their dogs are force-fed. I got two veggie tacos at Bull Taco, very delicious. We went to the juice place, bought two juices for then, two for later, and I got some crazy raw collard green wrap for later. I drove us back to the city, towards home, but we had to stop at Whole Foods first for some more supplies. We bought lots of vegetables, you wanted to hold the heavy handcart, but I knew you wouldn't want to for long. Somehow we bought wine, too. I can have one glass every three days. We bought two bottles. We made it back home. Somehow it was a busy day. K & R were glad to see us, jumping up and down. You were maybe a little grumpy from not eating anything all day. I had had those tacos. I ate my raw wrap, it tasted like a heap of flowers. I learned how to make hemp milk in the Vitamix, with the help of the internet. I looked everywhere online for an oldie for us to watch and I found one, highly recommended: *The Young in Heart*, which sounds off, but golden oldie con family with Douglas Fairbanks Jr., you fell asleep right away, but I will catch you up.

JULY 30, 2014

Yesterday I wrote my yesterday without you. This is the first time we've written yesterdays apart. At home, the ritual breaks.

Yesterday it was 3:00. It was hardly even a day. I do think 3pm is the most sensible time to wake up. I'm really not a daytime doll.

What? What am I supposed to say? We drove to La Jolla. We got a juice.

We drove home. We tried to deposit a check from SPD but we didn't have a pen in the car to sign it. I freaked out. What kind of people don't have a pen in the car. I try to keep us in pens. I take pride in my kits.

Yesterday I freaked out. You put a bag of coffee in a puddle of water and left it. You treated me like the child you think I am.

We went to Whole Foods where the chic go to buy their prepared meals. We got produce — kale, apples, tomatoes, strawberries, blueberries, raspberries, an avocado, two onions, one red one white. We tried not to buy too much, the co-op is better, I don't want to support the corporate ass.

Yesterday you found me the perfect classic movie with Douglas Fairbanks Jr. I fell asleep while Douglas Fairbanks Jr. and his teeth and his sister were friending or conning an old woman who fell asleep on her pillow, face framed in the frame, hair braided, neck tucked, saying, I won't be lonely anymore. A Scotsman suitor delightfully drops his words, each end inexistent.

He has the perfect Scottish name I can't remember.

Yesterday the Black and Chicana feminist texts I borrowed from the library were declared lost.

Yesterday I Facebooked Jaryd who was once my student now the IT guy to see if he could get me a new password. I got locked out of my account. He did. He also told me about meeting one of his favorite writers at Comic Con and finishing a story.

Yesterday I found you eating your cabbage leaf wrap in your studio at the computer. So blue. I was fasting. I watched you eat two hominy tacos at Bull Taco.

The first thing I did yesterday morning was ravage a piece of wedding cake with pineapple chunks, walking around the yard and house eating pineapple chunk wedding cake and frosting. I couldn't stop. I was an animal in my face.

I made vegan dog food, which only one dog would eat. I ordered vegan dog food online. Yesterday I single-handedly put to death the beef industry.

Yesterday Carmen and I texted to see if we could meet. But then her daughter was sick. Maybe breakfast.

Yesterday you called Radiology to schedule the PET scan. You got cut off twice. The receptionist was clearly fucked up. The bureaucracy was causing cancer. Finally she got you scheduled and gave you a list of instructions like, Don't be around children for six hours beforehand. But I think she meant after, because of the radiation. Eat a meal with protein the day before. Hydrate. Don't exercise.

I looked up PET scans on my phone to see the pros and cons. The doctor is not recommending it.

Yesterday you called Dr. Faries and talked to Dr. Lee about your slides. They still haven't seen the original lesion. Based on the slides of the lymph node, they are still recommending complete lymph node removal surgery. Still. He can see why you might want the PET scan. Now we're not so sure.

We don't want the surgery, we don't want anything. I read a post on a melanoma forum from a girl named Trixie or something who just wants to pretend it never happened. She's like a girl in a horror film opening the closet.

You called Dr. Brouha and left a message. He was in Yuma for the day.

I didn't eat anything except for the cake. I drank a berry juice, a coconut juice, a carrot juice. My body hurt all over.

THREE

JULY 31, 2014

Yesterday I am going to try to chronicle like you are. Are you? Are you using sound? Are you making images? Are you playing like with peas? Are you breaking
lines?

Yesterday slow. We seem to have sides of bed after 10 years. Seem. I have a stack of books that includes Michael Davidson, Sally Banes, *Letters to Poets*.

Text from Carmen. We'll breakfast with poet friends and kids. I am glad she's slow. There is no way I can make anywhere before 10am.

I shower for some reason. I never shower. Never in the morning either. I wash my hair. I condition. I don't shave. I let my armpits go. I oil up.

I think I wash some dishes. I make a pot of oolong tea in the white Swedish teapot. I decant the tea into the metal carafe. I combine homemade vegan dog food with meaty dog kibble. You feed Kiki by hand. She spits out each green bean.

I get dressed. I wear my new thrift black ankle moccasins but they jingle when I walk, who do I think I am. I strap them up. I wear a tie-dyed black and white tube skirt that is really blue and white. I like how high it goes up, I could wear this thing to my shoulders. It could be a great tube dress without boobs.

I hug Carmen. We sit at a picnic bench table in the middle of the restaurant.

When we walk in she and her two loves sit on one side of the bench with devices each. Like a portrait. Sophia watches Scooby-Doo. Jackson plays some jet pack game. I am sure you wish you could play.

Does the same rule apply about photographing children as writing about them? I need a release form.

I am an exhaust I
need to stop when
we get home

We listen to the Buffalo Bills. We walk the dogs to the park, around the block, past the pinecones.

Later I write your file. Later we see Rae & Chuck. Later we watch Michel Gondry from the back of the Ken theater. Recalling these days is its own exhaust.

Carmen recalls her visit to Cuba with Ed Hirsch. Her trip to Peru. The drive from Las Cruces with kids. Jackson navigates. Evan stays home to finish book. Sophia is sick. Carmen tells us about it.

We tell her about melanoma. A little bit. I am afraid to say the word cancer in front of the kids. Like I always cuss in front of kids. Like I told the joke about Phuckphace and Bitch Lips in front of my niece. I am relieved when Carmen cusses.

We talk about the trauma of writing, the trauma of writing post trauma. How everything else is a joke.

Rae and Chuck recall their five weeks in Italy, four at Bellagio. They tell us about the UN guy and the prime minister guy and the Iranian woman activist and an engineer from Duke. They are transformed.

We ride the red scooter to the restaurant. When we pass Rae & Chuck's street I think, I bet they walked. They always drive, but I bet, after Italy, they walked.

When we get to the restaurant they tell us they walked. There is something glowing about Rae & Chuck, something internally relaxed and undone. They laugh a lot in the movie across the street. They laugh a lot at the dinner. We don't talk too much about Melanoma. They tell us their stories of their days.

We tell Rae & Chuck & Carmen about our failed self-residency in Mendocino, how we left five days early.

You and I share a carafe of house red. We share a salad and mushroom raviolis. We eat fresh wheat bread and soft whipped butter.

When we get home, I have a headache either from the jaw or the temple or the wine. We try to watch the rest of *The Young in Heart*. Douglas Fairbanks Jr. looks like a redhead in color.

The Scot's name is Duncan.

I am trying to be better about seeing people.

07.31.2014

Yesterday up early, guilty about skipping my workout, went down to the basement at 7:30 and stumbled through, the house was alive when I came back up. We had social plans throughout the day, meeting Carmen at Great Maple at 10:15, so she confirmed on your phone via text, I made a reservation online before we split. A few minutes getting some of my files together for the tenure package, and then we drove over. Right on time but they were already there, I didn't need my reservation, but told the hostess so I wouldn't get flack from Opentable.com. She was there without Evan, but with her two kids. They were both on iPads, but were present nonetheless. They were beautiful kids, funny, and we had a kind of central table. I want to describe these places sometime, but it seems beside the point. What will I say, hipster remodeled Denny's with brasserie flair? We had our breakfast: I didn't want to order the sexpot tea out loud, but that's what I wanted so I did. You had tea too, we ordered collectively as always, they had new items—better for our lifestyle now! Vegan hash and I had the avocado toast with fruit. They have a kid's menu, I did not know that. Organic things. We used to get it all, cocktails, the bacon donuts on the walk-by plank, I'd eat until my feet hurt. Carmen was great at conversation, I felt like I hadn't spoken to anyone in a while, anyone but you, and I can grunt at you and you know what I mean, I felt like I hadn't spoken a language I barely knew in years and here I was at Great Maple trying to speak with a genius. Carmen, you, the kids, the hash was good, the toast was good. The boy looked like Evan and Carmen, he had long curls and a Yankee hat, the girl was cool and funny, but had been sick all week. Carmen talked about how they had been on the road, letting Evan finish a book, how they work, the difficulty, about her mom, etc. She is our friend. We spoke about our situation, the desert house, my cancer, our plans, etc. We talked and ate. She told us about going to Cuba with Ed Hirsch, how he was still stuck on the Language poets, how they took over and destroyed his poetry world, how it's a travesty that the Cuban poets are translating Duncan rather than Bishop, how they will get the wrong idea down there. She told us about the Language anthology circulating in carbon copy in Cuba, the ripples outward. She showed us a picture of trees growing from the walls of a palace. She told us about Daniel's newest controversy, Cheap Signaling and the Marxist contest, how someone online called him a, what was it, a puke or something. Anne Boyer? We talked, left, the son put his arm around me for a picture. I almost wept, or something. We came home, worked on my file, me on the bibliography, you on the letter, great teamwork, we're getting somewhere now. Those hours stacked up, I moved one item from one category to another. I made us some nutbutter in the Vitamix, we had it with carrots. You wrote and we asked each other questions. I will thank you here tomorrow as well. Thank you here now. We had plenty left to do, but it was evening, time to ride the scooter to meet Rae and Chuck at Blue Boheme, to hear about her trip to Italy, her week at some school run by a pot impresario who didn't pay her or Paul, who was also there and who needed the cash for his mortgage. Then they went on to the Bellagio residency, which blew their minds—they walked to the Boheme, big deal there, and they told us about the world leaders they met there, someone from the head of the United Nations told them that when the ocean rises 2 cm all of Florida will be struck by dengue fever, effectively killing 6% or was it 60% of the population, how the guy cannot even use the words global warming. How Hilary Clinton started to talk about elephants to another dude and he didn't know why until another dude told him that Hilary was visiting China and saw massive elephant death. How the dude told the Chinese ambassador that he didn't want his country to be known as the one that made elephants extinct. We told Rae and Chuck about our doctors, about the decisions we are balancing right now (PET scan, remove all my lymph nodes in my groin), about our trip up and down the coast, about the desert. We went across the street to the Ken to see a movie, what was it, *Mood Indigo* by Michel Gondry. The Ken is the perfect theater, one screen only, and that was the perfect movie. I don't care what anyone says.

AUGUST 1, 2014

Yesterday I wrote your tenure file. I'm not supposed to say that. You're not supposed to have stress. I'm good at writing files. I have to be.

I procrastinated by doing other things first. Closing out my account from my grandmother from 1999. Calling the Angels foster baby project. They don't have a packet but they do have an orientation. Elizabeth told me in a message.

I made a list of all the 1913 submissions who need books sent. This is grueling and secretarial. I can't take it anymore. I can't stop.

Yesterday we talked about the yesterday project. We're not supposed to talk about it. We talked about how it gets boring sometimes. We said style is suicide. Or shame.

Kelly from Dr. Faries' office called to make sure someone had called us. Kelly is the only one who calls. Kelly saved us. Kelly hopes we had a good vacation, time to get away, not be on machines. I love Kelly.

Yesterday I drank so much water. Infused with strawberries and lemon. You made me a chocolate hemp milkshake while I wrote file.

We finally finished the Douglas Fairbanks Jr. film. One of these women has been in a Western. We agree the best scene is the one we re-watch, where the father-son grifter pair watch the men working on a construction site.

They don't understand why they do it. They note how passionate some of the men are, lugging one sack from one place to another, and then back again. It's biology, says the father, the Sahib. Some men are drawn to carry sacks from one spot to another.

Sahib and Mommy they are called, as if it's unusual or acceptable. Mommy sounds like Mawmy. Maybe that was a radical name once. Once I met a girl named Santa. No I didn't meet her, but I heard of her. We all feel this way about Santa.

I wrote straight from 2 to 8. Tallying the numbers was the worst. The biobib is the worst. You could have done it but it would have taken weeks. And horror. No one should have to write such a thing about themselves anyway. It's much easier to talk about other people.

We chatted online and plinked each other and sent faces from the front of the house to the back. It got too hot to work in the sunroom.

Ronald Johnson lay on the slate under my desk but freaked out at a dog walking by and smashed my bum knee. I banished Ronald Johnson.

You made pasta with mushrooms and we drank rabbit wine.

I fell asleep early but woke up after a dream including Mark Levine and Emily Wilson. They were on my mind and in my dream. Then there was another part I can't remember. I couldn't sleep and did nothing about it.

The tone of these is getting truly abyssal. I've got to try something else.

Oh now I'm back to add a few things, it's only been a couple minutes so that still seems within rules of game. What are the rules.

I'm not sure you could have written the tenure file. Should I say that I've written every job letter, every CV of yours. I have ways of not feeling all 1950s housewife about this. For instance, I like to yell a lot. I don't cook. You clean too, although I'm better at it. You do laundry. You did laundry all day while I wrote the document. Every publication, every single reading, every class, every scrap of "service." These terms negate each other. They negate us. No wonder you got cancer, you were everyone's bitch. You didn't say no. We sat in a car waiting for your student once for an hour because she needed a form signed. I almost punched everyone. That was when you already had cancer. I punch cancer.

I remember several couples in the neighborhood growing up—the wife had literally written the husband's Ph.D. dissertation, and of course he left for some young shippie later, left her with kids and house. We survive by self-advertisement. Some of us know how to make a thing look us. Some of us who know that are females. Some of us know how to make a man look good.

There is a pile of straight white male bullshit in here, but it has not gone unaccounted for between us. I've said it many times and you've at least heard me say it, if not understood completely. You get given shit because of your penis. Also, yes you're nice and white and tall and unthreatening at the same time. There's a whole package ok.

People automatically assume I'm either insane, stupid, or fuckable/rapeable. So I've gotten good at writing prose for bureaucracies, telling them how fucking great I am, how uninsane, unstupid, and unfucked. I don't even mention blond.

It's the same thing as women and minorities getting lower student evaluations. Of course the systems base everything on evaluations now. Let the freaks in, but give 'em hell. Make them want to leave. Make everything harder.

So I write your tenure letter so you can get the raise so I can work less and write more and you can cook and clean and make the big bucks so we can take a vacation or go to the desert with the dogs or have a little kid someday so you don't die. Ok?

08.01.2014

Yesterday I got up a little earlier, looked around, made some tea, looked at the internet. It's a little fuzzy. The whole day was devoted to my tenure file, searching out the things I'd done, handing them over to you to put in prose, you've volunteered because you're so much faster, your prose is so much more clear. And you can organize a document, put it tight so it works, whereas I can barely write about yesterday. That's what we did. There were smoothies early, beans and quinoa later, and pasta and mushrooms much later. I tried to ply you with treats and chores: bagging up 1913 orders, laundry, cooking, smiling, but we'd saved this job and it was a two-person one. I updated my biobib, CV, and put together the other documents we needed. I fed you the info just as you needed it, or a few minutes earlier. I searched my email for dates and proper names. I found my student evaluations, which I hadn't read before, and teared up at some of their praise. I sent you these. It seemed like I'd done quite a bit in the three categories: research, teaching, and service, at least to me. But this school has never had a poet go up for tenure before, that's what they tell me. We kind of worked together, but you wrote it, you wrote it, you wrote it, thank you, I love you, you told me you would do it and now you were doing it and I was ashamed but knew how much better you would do and how much quicker and that it would hurt to do it, really hurt to go back over all of that, those years, those things we're blaming the cancer on, though it can't be that can it, it can't be the job, though the things we were detailing were stressful, even to see them again. You didn't burn me on it, either, you said you were having fun but how could it be, who likes to do such things, but there it was and that's what we did. My favorite evaluation was the one that said "there are so many awesome poems

91

out there," or the many that said I was passionate about poetry, which are my favorites because it means I'm a good actor, I am passionate, I guess, about poetry when it means something, when the kids are staring at me, when I want it to matter to them, to me, to anyone, anything more than what matters in this world. But most poetry is pretty boring. Some of the evaluators thought they were filling out a rate-my-professors kind of thing, where they were giving future students the key to passing the class, which of course isn't the point at all. I loved reading your praise of me in my voice, the document growing, listing my accomplishments, all 11 pages of them, how overqualified I am, but how under too, how many great poets there are out there, just like me, great on their own free way, no one knows what they are saying, or if they work at all, no one reads them, not even me, but I will get tenure thanks to you, my darling. It took all day but we did it, you did it, I couldn't find all the books we need to send, no copies of CA's book, one copy of the journal, the pasta was really good, I put the boiling water in the sauce and it tasted excellent, we ate it all, no exercise all day, we did talk about this project a little bit, maybe we'll read it at the reading we agreed to do with the cool kiddoes, hear what each other thinks of our days, our days. We watched the rest of *The Young in Heart* in bed and we were seriously transfixed. There's a scene where the father and son (Doug Fairbanks) watch the workers like ants, wondering what the pleasure is in carrying those heavy bags from the one pile to the other over and over. In the end, Miss Fortune drives the Wombat and moves in with the Con Artists, who have all found the glory of work. Everyone gets promoted, everyone is in love.

AUGUST 2, 2014

Yesterday needs an edit. But that's outside the bounds of yesterday. What happens in yesterday becomes today.

I'll start with Gustavo. Señor Gustavo at Romesco in Bonita by the border. There is one best waiter and one best restaurant and these are them. They exceed their categories, excel the vegetable. Gustavo is old with a moustache that should be pronounced moose-tash-a. He winks. For some reason we always get him, maybe because Gustavo goes over big with gringos. I try my Spanish on him, which is always a controversial choice. My Spanish works.

We remember one of our last trips to Romesco with Ryan Hand and Sarah Baker when we had a large coupon and made it even larger, ordering $25 mescal shots for all of us and one for Gustavo. He brought over the enormous oversized mescal bottle, it took an entire man to carry it. This was pre-cancer when we did this kind of thing on a Tuesday night.

No mescal yesterday. One glass of red blend from the Guadalupe Valley. Not the salty one, but excellent. We order the Romesco tomato soup, the Roquefort salad, two Gobernador tacos, mushrooms in garlic sauce, a baby quail, grilled, and a plate of marinated garlics. I say we're eating Hopsy when we eat the quail. You say eat the bones.

Yesterday your parents come to town. Apparently they fly in, get a car at Avis, and go to their hotel. We don't know what hotel. They text us. We wait to get lunch with them. Then they text us that they're already eating at a restaurant. We say some things just between us. Then we realize this is better and we eat our quinoa and black beans at home. We write our yesterdays. We walk the dogs to the park and around the block. We tell your parents to come over. Maybe your parents are afraid to eat with us or don't want to eat what we eat. To the beat. Maybe they are just trying to be low maintenance. I say there's nothing more high maintenance than pretending to be low maintenance.

They are at the Lafayette Hotel with the famous Johnny Weissmuller almost-Olympic-sized pool but they didn't bring their bathing suits. Your sister is here, we find out when she gets out of the car.

We sit and talk with your parents and your sister Meredith. I sit on the floor with the dogs. Then I sit in a chair. You sit on the bench with Meredith. Then you sit in a chair. Then I sit on the floor again. Then Meredith sits in a chair. I bring out glasses of water infused with strawberries. They seem to understand the horror.

Then we walk around the house and go outside. We show them the outdoor shower, the studio room, the renovated canned ham Shasta trailer with wings. We sit around the outdoor table. You lay in the hammock. I sit on a tiny red backless bench at a corner, almost under you. In the shade. Your parents sit in the sun and don't move to the shade. It seems like they want shade but they don't move into the shade.

Your mom is yawning and wants to go back to the hotel. I tell your parents about the Pizzeria Luigi by their hotel. Your dad wants to try some of our recipes, make hemp milk and nut butters from scratch and try the blender. We talk about war-mongering and money. Your dad wants to kill bankers with his own personal drone. Your mom tells us about the goddess Cuba statue in Sorrento, Italy, protector of children, the name of their town. They bring their town everywhere they go. Meredith is going to open a fudge shop in the opera house called Elmer Fudge.

After your parents leave, we go to the drive-in. First to Romesco and then to the drive-in by the beach. I am bad at chronology. First I make popcorn to bring in a big wooden bowl. The popcorn sits on the back seat in a wooden bowl, covered by two cotton blue and white striped napkins. I am bad at order.

Defenders of the Universe, I mean, *Guardians of the Galaxy*. There are three girls in it. They don't talk to each other not about men. I get bored in the fight scenes, but I like the settings like Maxfield Parrish backgrounds. We are surrounded by kids who get in for $1.00. At the end of the movie, one of them keeps shouting, "She's lying!" when the hero is finally opening the package from his dead mother. It's Awesome Mix Tape II. There will be a sequel, we will find out who his father is. There are references to *Footloose* and Bowie songs.

Your parents make me want to be nicer. I am trying to be nicer. This is almost impossible.

08.02.2014

Yesterday my parents were coming to town and I hadn't spoken to them in forever and they aren't great communicators and I'm a terrible communicator but they were coming, we thought, around eleven. Flying from Buffalo. I set my alarm but I woke up first, went straight to the basement to exercise because it would be a full day. I came upstairs soaked in sweat, changed my shirt but you were up and you told me to change it again. We had to clean the whole house, naturally, though it was pretty good, certainly cleaner than my parent's house when we visit that, but we had to do it and we did. You told me where to direct my cleanliness and we kept rolling. My dad texted me from Arizona at 9:30, that gave us, maybe, 'til noon. At 11 I took the car to wash the desert dust off, and to vacuum it out. It was a mess but I cleaned it pretty good. I got 10 dollars' worth of tokens and used all the various settings. I felt terrible about the drought, about the suds flowing down the drain. It was muggy for San Diego, my shirt was soaked again. I made it back home and had a text from my dad. They had landed, had a car. My phone rang, it was VW to schedule our 30,000-mile tune-up. I scheduled it for a time we won't be here, when I asked to change it, she said it was already in the system. You were annoyed. I was rude to the lady on the phone. I asked my dad where they were staying. All on text. The Lafayette, good four blocks away. I said why don't you come over if you can't get into the hotel. Ok, he said. But they weren't coming over. I could tell you were hungry, I made us smoothies. We drank our smoothies and appreciated our clean home. We thought we'd get some lunch with them, researched the options. Texted them about lunch. They were already having lunch. What was going on here? You said it was passive-aggressive, I thought it was passive-passive, what's the difference, aggression is just whatever you think it is. So we wrote back that we were going to eat and we ate some leftovers. We said come on over and finally they did. They had my sister Meredith with them, which wasn't a surprise but still I didn't really know if she was coming. They came in the door and R & K went insane, I didn't know how to get them to cool it. They were jumping, crying, barking. I grabbed them by the collars and made them get on the floor. Then they started being really good and we got to see my parents. I could see you enjoying their company. I got more relaxed. I watched you talk to them, enjoyed your profile in the light, your humor, your grace. We kept going back to the subject, to the big C, explaining to them the plan and what it means. It doesn't mean anything, there's nothing but confidence and hope that the lifestyle change will keep the life going on. We just kind of hung out here. They are good parents, they love us. Their politics are good. You got them water and told them it was special because it had strawberries in it. A water cocktail. We told them about the diet, all this pressure on the diet, but it's all we have. It's something to point to. We chatted, heard their stories, told them part of ours. They were so sleepy, three hours of jetlag but they also got up really early to get to the airport. They went back to the hotel after three hours or so, no snacks, we recommended Luigi's, and they drove back after hugs, but we still had energy to burn so we went to Romesco and had our perfect night, really, incredible food in Bonita with our favorite waiter Gustavo who is our best friend and we held back on the ordering which was perfect so we still had room for the popcorn you made at the drive-in and we even got to the drive-in early and it was a lovely evening, with the moon hovering over the screen as we enjoyed the summer blockbuster *Guardians of the Galaxy*, which is your new favorite movie.

AUGUST 3, 2014

Yesterday Fudgamacallit. Yesterday Fudgegettaboutit. Yesterday Mother Fudger.

Everything takes so long. I think we wake up. I think we go to bed. I read Rosa Alcalá's *Undocumentaries*. I have hated poetry for so long, this seems pretty good. I can't say anything more about that.

We pick up your parents and sister at the hotel. We drive them around through traffic. It rains in San Diego. We know this is good. It rains hard when we are farthest from the car.

A youngish girl picks green berries off a tree and throws them by the handful into the bay in front of us. I am the only one who notices. She and I smile at each other, I think. I am pretty sure of that.

Your parents notice a splash in the water behind us and wonder what the sound was. I tell them about the girl. But not everything.

There is a large family reunion type thing going on in the park beside us. Everyone wears blue identifying t-shirts. They sit at tables, they cook on grills, they have canopies. There may be another group too.

We turn around and it starts raining hardest. A man on a bicycle says, There is a sidewalk. This means we're supposed to walk where the walking happens. We walk there.

My red shoes soak through. I have two scarves I left in the car. We get back in the car. I am smashed in the middle between your mother and your sister. Your mother takes a while getting in the car. Your sister and I wait in the rain.

In the hotel earlier, your father gives you a black rolled up cloth. You unroll it. It's a gold dagger with a ship on it. A letter opener. For larger things. Later I open a few letters with it. It's too powerful for regular mail. How did he get it on the plane, everyone says. Your mother is lying down with her feet up trying to get her sandals on.

We take them to lunch at the vegan place for carnivores. It's a stretch. Your sister tries my tofu. They all get fountain drinks. We get hot tea. They get fake meat and French fries.

We go to Cabrillo point and the visitor's center and the statue and the view in the rain which is no view. Your father says the view needs Visine. We read about the maps and the clothes and the food on the galleons. One Spaniard is tried for cruelty to the Native Americans. He is found not guilty.

There are maybe some adopted kids in here. Lots of kids, many interested. That seems doable. I want a book of the National Parks. I want to camp.

We drive your father to the ship replica and he gets out to take pictures. We stay in the car where it's raining.

We drop them back at the hotel for siesta and we go to the grocery. We both notice one of your colleagues there but we don't tell each other until later. We don't say hi to each other, us and the colleague, maybe the colleague didn't see us. We haven't seen any colleagues since the cancer, it's going to be too awkward. It's always awkward to spell awkward.

You make vegan chili and cornbread from scratch with no sugar. I make a veggie plate. You make hummus. Your parents and your sister come over. We get the dogs to stay on the floor by cruelty. We listen to Andre Reed's Hall of Fame speech on your phone. The jazz station plays heavy blues.

We watch four *Louie*'s after they go. The *Louie*'s give me hope for writing, for this form. I'm doing it all wrong.

In the morning I looked at the yard and thought about what I wanted. All I wanted was to go to the co-op by the beach. I wanted to go to that place. But it will have to wait.

08.03.2014

Yesterday my parents were here when we got up, at the Lafayette, we needed to eat all day, we needed a plan, the plan was to get breakfast separately and then call them up, to do things, to eat meals. I worked out first thing, made us tea and smoothies. You fed the dogs their new V-dog vegan dog food with all the supplements, with the garlic (I've read dogs are allergic to garlic, but this company says not so), the green goo, the sweet potato. I showered outside and we dressed to meet them. We saw their hotel room, the remodel was working, nice room, small, but fine. Just fine. I wished I could stay there, watch TV for the rest of my life, pull the covers over my head, anonymously. You were great with them. We were going to go to the harbor to look at boats. What were these strange gray things in the sky? I drove us down, Saturday: Everyone had the same idea. There wasn't a spot to park in the city. Traffic was so slow. My dad told us about his new friend who donated a 17th century piano to the opera house my dad rebuilt in his tiny town. How this guy collects strange instruments, how he plays the glass harmonica, how this piano was tossed in with a calliope he bought in Chicago. How he just dropped it off. How my dad had to find a tuner. How he did, just at the last moment. How the tuner said it was the finest piano he'd seen in a while. How a player mechanism had been installed in the '70s. MIDI. Cassette tapes. How you can hook that up to Bluetooth now. How he also got two monster movie screens from neighborhood schools. How he inherited hundreds of chairs from the closing churches in his rundown town. I could see you in the back, you, my mom, my sister, you in the middle, no room for you at all. It was a nice drive, but everyone wanted these spaces! It was a land war. I drove us away, to Spanish Landing, where there were spots.

We took a little walk, towards the boat they are rebuilding, the one my dad saw eight months ago. One drop fell from the sky, more, more. We are in the worst drought in history. The sky opened up, we turned around. We were soaked, all of us. I gave you my hat and ran to get the car. The drops were enormous. I hadn't been in, or seen rain in so long. It ruined our plans, but it was rain, it was what the world needed. I drove us to Naked Café, a splurge nutritionally but all vegan versions of things Americans like. I got the seitan Reuben. It was good, but I can't care anymore. My parents ate their healthy food, didn't complain. We told them about Monsanto, about the way they crop-bombed Mexican growers to make them rely on their chemicals. They were down for the fight, but I can't see it. Not sure they liked their food. Not sure I liked my food, but it was comforting. We drove to Cabrillo monument, best view in the city but it was so cloudy, you could barely see anything. First place Spanish settlers landed on the west coast of CA. We went in the museum, to see how they handled the genocide thing. Not so well, but there were newer placards that spoke a bit to the experience. The disease, a population of 25 million cut to 3 million in 75 years. Not a lot of apology in the diction, not a lot of sensitivity. Conquistadors, explorers, what if you find something and you fuck it up. There was zero view, the fog following us everywhere. I liked the maps though, the way that they filled in the places they didn't know anything about with serpents and imaginary creatures. I liked the astrolabe, and the pegboard you tabulated your nautical twists and turns on. It looked like a little game. We dropped the family off at the hotel for a siesta, went to Sprouts to get groceries, marveled at how almost all the bulk was conventional, especially for a store capitalizing on the natural healthy buzz. I have cancer! I kept returning to it in talks to my parents, making light of it, poking it with my tongue. I cooked vegan chili, vegan cornbread, called them up, come on down. We hung out, I had the NFL Hall of Fame induction speeches on my phone, I wanted to hear Andre Reed, childhood hero, hear him talk. Something was lost without the optics. We had fun, invented names for their fudge store. I think I won, Fudgegeddiboutit, but I liked your variations on Fuck: Fudge you, Fudge off, Motherfudger's, etc. They were sleepy early, so were we, they went home, I looked up Andre's speech on the internet, it had actually been a beautiful event. The city might lose its team, really the only thing there, their owner had died, the team was for sale, and their best quarterback ever had cancer. He threw Andre a pass after his speech. I wept. We went to bed but watched four episodes of *Louie* first. The man is doing things with narrative that have never been attempted.

AUGUST 4, 2014

Yesterday I'm still amazed there was one. Angela Davis & Rosa Alcalá in bed. Chris Kraus is or isn't the grand niece of Karl Kraus. But she should be. We were late as usual. You got in a bad frame. The moods of having your parents in town. We took them to the farmer's market, which your father called "eye opening." Hand-massaged rabbits and the mushroom guy. All organic creams and cheeses. Pea juice. Your mother and sister filled up on free samples. A woman playing a violin stomped out on a board with taps. We parked near the Catholic church where your mother walked to mass. She walked the hill straight up Polk Avenue, said she'd never been in a place with so much diversity, she told us the race of everyone, which she called descent, sounds like dissent. Walked by a multi-colored van with Hakuna Matata painted on the back. Is that or isn't that a saying outside *The Lion King*. Discuss. We ducked back in for squash and a chocolate brown hot pepper from Suzie's stand. Your parents stopped to look at metal objects made out of keys for grandson Lincoln, who is key-obsessed. We walk by two different homeless men sleeping on the sidewalk. Your dad seems impressed that you can sleep anywhere in this town. Do you give them money or would they be insulted. We come back to the house with the dogs. We try the new method of pushing Kiki over to stop her jumping. It works. She is slightly insulted, just enough. I give out water with a raspberry in it, water cocktails. We get hungry. Walk to the Mission, where it's too busy to wait. I realize too late this is more walking than maybe they are used to. We walk to Rancho's. The regular things like waiting and ordering become pressured with other people. I am trying to manage being around other people. I wonder how long I could go without wanting to see any. Months. Your father orders the El

Healthy burrito. He is in solidarity. Your mother and sister get a fish burrito and a salmon burrito. You get a bowl. I get the vegan enchilada trio in the colors of the flag of Mexico. I pay too much attention to the chips, each piece. We get the special habanero salsas. You don't get any corn tortillas, although you ask twice. We get too full. We walk back to our house and your dad suggests a hotel siesta. Good plan. We drive them back and drop them off. Then we drive home. Then I siesta on the couch. You look at the Buffalo Bills. We try to get the Hall of Fame game on the laptop but it's blacked out. We dog-proof the furniture with laptops and books and turn on the jazz station for them. Kiki is pissed, it's gray and rainy, it's our fault. I don't want to forget about the dogs if there's a baby. The dogs are depressed. They eat their combo-vegan/combo-bison kibble. We give them a sweet potato, a kong, a greenie. We go to the hotel. Your mother finds us on the stairs coming up from the garage. She always finds us, she always appears. We sit in the restaurant, they've made a friend who turns on the game. We don't want to order, so we all go to the room. Meredith is pissed, her back hurts. She walks back to the lobby with her pink purse. We watch the game. Your mom makes a joke about having twins named Silas and Cyrus. I say she would have octuplets at her age. You nudge me, she laughs. She comes up with all the names for the octuplets. The last one is Silo. What about Sinus, now I think. She says the best part is naming them anyhow. When we get home I'm supposed to pick a movie while you work out. Instead I research the foster baby program. You can get a really tiny one. But you might have to give it back. That seems like my old invention, the borrow-a-baby library. It doesn't sound too bad, it sounds terrible, it could be doable. You pick a movie, we watch *Super*. I make popcorn and cantaloupe, you make an apple and nut butter. We drink water cocktails. We told your parents to check out the Red Fox room, brought from England intact by Marion Davies. We say the French fries are good, and the whiskeys, and the piano bar. We used to go there all the time.

08.04.2014

Yesterday I woke up mad, angry at things, at my body, at the obvious, everything about me, this little parental visit across the country with nothing to do, the awkwardness, the foreverness of this, the way you are forced to root for it to last as long as it can, the kind of thinking that this will get me, someday, as far off as I can make it. I was in a bad mood. I made us a bad smoothie. Too many things. I didn't care. I drank it in one gulp. I hated it. Or maybe you were in a bad mood and I copied you, I don't know. My parents and M were in town and we needed to have a good day. I texted them an ETA, we'd be by at 10 or so. We cleaned ourselves, I tried to shake it off. Or maybe it was the seasonal affective disorder, no sun for two days, the great smells of drought-tolerant rain on the ground. Or maybe it was the obligation, the planning, the need to do things when what would we do? But the parents were understanding, just a little helpless, no real motive but to be present. And you were fantastic, offering suggestions, making suggestions, smiling, laughing. We stumbled to the hotel, I knew they'd been awake for hours. Rather, we drove to their hotel room, I knew they'd been awake for hours. We took them to the farmer's market, showed them the people, the energy, the good food fresh from the ground, the crafts, the woman playing her fiddle and stomping on her wood. We bought green juice, some vegetables, farmer's market things. It was still gray overhead, but ok. We went to our house, sat around, but not until after I shoved the dogs to the ground during their greetings. It worked with K, we shall have to explore this method further. We had the same chats we had had before, more about my parent's adventures in their small town. I tried to get my sister to talk, my poor sister, looking so old now, so enormously hunched, so much trouble in her life, her syndrome, her job of ten years, putting the caps on travel mugs. I thought about my parents, how they have housed their daughter for 39 years, how she is incapable of independence, how she knows this, how it tortures her. My mom mentioned some people she thought I knew but I didn't. I only spoke about nutrition, how all I can do is keep my body together. Someone mentioned that when I was a kid my teacher had called me a word-attacker. I could tell you were hungry. Even I was. We walked to Rancho's, I had a bowl of food but forgot to get the brown rice and black beans. You got the vegan enchilada trio but ditto on the rhythm and blues. My family ate their tubes of goo. I ate my bowl. It was swell. It was two hours to game time! We dropped them off at their hotel for a siesta, we went home for one. The Bills were playing in an hour, we'd planned to go to the Bills bar and watch them, but I was not feeling it. Thought I could get it through my subscription to Preseason Live, but the Hall of Fame Game was blacked out. We only had a few minutes before game time, you texted my parents to see if they could get the game. They saved the day! It was on in the hotel when we got there, such sweet relief. We prostrate on their bed and watching the scrubs. I have an analysis of the game but will not bore you, it's more about the function of preseason as commodity. Why do I watch this? Because of being raised near where the team was, because I need a nerdy obsession. It's a terrible world and this is my way to live. We watched, often in silence. We were all chairman of the bored, but we were present in each other's presence. We went home, got stoned, watched a movie on Netflix, *Super*.

AUGUST 5, 2014

Yesterday is becoming painful for you. You dread writing yesterdays. You are a word-attacker, your father told us that your 2nd grade teacher said that. Ben is a Word-Attacker.

I am not going to try to shine this up into something. Yesterday we fell asleep watching the Roger Ebert documentary. It's painful to watch him exist without a jaw. I don't want you thinking this is going to happen to you. It could happen to me. It happens.

Yesterday we did Pilates in the living room, then we went to the Angels Foster orientation. The horror of sitting in a room with other people. We didn't really belong there, we don't like families. We certainly don't want to grow one. But borrowing babies doesn't sound so bad, I think. You think, Why would you want to borrow a kid at their worst, when they're screaming. I try to tell you about crying, that the problem is usually solvable. It's not until they're two or three that they really scream for no reason. Then you put them in day care.

Maybe we're not cut for this. I keep thinking of the time clock, well it's only 20 years or so and then we can have our life back. It's only a few years before they go to school. Maybe that's the wrong way to think about it.

We sent your parents and sister off down Washington to the Avis then to the airport. We took them to Great Maple first. I had the asparagus with parmesan and poached egg. You had avocado toast. They had loads of bacon and coffee. We paid for it all.

Yesterday I walked around the house a lot. I fell asleep in the studio where you were working. Then you fell asleep next to me. Then it got too hot. Too many flies in the air.

If only yesterdays included recording the little sights of a day, like two people biking uphill on a tandem past our door, which just happened now, but that's today. Or someone in pink shorts carrying a pink and green surfboard, walking. Just now.

We parked in the red and too close to a car behind us. The guy was lucky we came back. We moved our car to let him out. That's yesterday.

I missed our neighborhood driving around when it was right in front of me. I dreaded another trip.

We talked for hours about the baby-kid thing. Maybe we'll just try to save the $30,000 to buy one. We could make one but we don't see the point in that. It's not environmentally responsible. I said we should try to talk about it instead of just saying, Fuck it, and jumping in, like we usually do. You said, It's not fuck it.

You wanted to know what the connection is between your cancer and the baby thing. I had a lot of answers for that. I don't know what your answer is for that. I hardly care about anything.

You heated up some chili and quinoa and we drank the rest of the rabbit Malbec. You were worried it might be bad for you. I said I didn't think so. I was worried that you were worried. You were worried about the melanoma coming back and what if it does and isn't it more stressful to have a baby-kid then. I agreed. But I thought we agreed to not worry about it coming back.

I explained to you my worry-to-relief ratio, that if you worry too much there is never any relief, even when the worry doesn't come true.

Is this banal? I didn't see anyone eating yogurt on a unicycle like we did the other day when we walked to Rancho's with your family. But that wasn't yesterday either. I didn't see a polka dotted kid on roller skates with a balloon on her head while feeding my orphan, the squirrel in Central Park.

You dropped off your manuscript at Rae's house and stayed for a while. Later you told me you both talked about your cancers and how you both felt fine even when something is wrong, even when the cancer was there, even when it's not. I'm not sure how this is supposed to comfort me. Maybe you're freaking out and worrying all the time about it coming back. Why am I not worried, or am I. I read something on my phone about how it's impossible to cure when it spreads to the lymph nodes. Irresponsible middle-America reporting. Are we going to do the PET scan? We don't talk about it.

I made us an orange smoothie with coconut water and coconut flakes and coconut butter and maca. Four oranges. Lots of ice. Right in the middle of yesterday.

There are so many things I forget to put in the yesterdays that would probably make better news.

08.05.2014

Yesterday we spoke a bit about this project, but later in the day, about who it could possibly be for, about the obligation, the vacancy, the things that are left out. Everything is left out. We do have sex. We do get mad. The project is not a project in complete transparency, rather, one in willful obfuscation. But we haven't decided this. The first rule of yesterday is no talking about the yesterday. We shied away from it. I was pissed to have to go over it again, a day with family, a day with so many banal frustrations, none that I wanted to elucidate. But that was later in the day. Earlier we woke, and started getting ready to see my parents off. First plan was breakfast at Great Maple. My dad started texting a bit early, I think they were worried about making it to the airport in time. I texted back, be there in half an hour. They had already pulled their car out when we got there, there was some anxiety. There was plenty of time. Needed to get the rental back to Avis before noon, it was 9:30. Ok. They followed me to Great Maple, but the lot was full. I parked half on the red, left them a nice spot two cars behind us. We had reservations. I had reservations. They had the table in the corner ready for us, the round one, you and I took the inner seats because everyone else would never have been able to slide in. I could tell they were shocked by the prices. There were so many creative items, but they all ordered the traditional breakfast. You got your asparagus, me the avocado toast. We talked and it got nice, just get them going on Cuba and it's ok. They said they may come out west again for the Rose Parade, I couldn't get Elliott Smith out of my head. The man who stabbed himself in the heart. You gave them the dates we'd be around as we'd planned, it seemed to scare my mom off. But we wanted to see them, couldn't we see them? My dad maneuvered and said yes, we'll see you then. Breakfast was over, time to roll. We pointed them towards Washington St., showed them how to get to the airport on the phone. They were ready. We all love each other. There was no ticket on my dash. We gathered around our cars, saying our loving goodbyes, hugs and kisses in the air. I saw a man approaching, a little pissed off, he asked me if this car was mine. I had clearly parked him in, clearly, terribly. I apologized profusely. He was nice about it. I was sorry. My family drove away, I could breathe a little bit better. We went home. I think we lay down, something happened. I remember, we took a nap in the studio, where I was printing out things to drop off at Rae's house, save her a trip to La Jolla. That's what I was doing. You came in, we took a nap on the pallet bed. I turned on the jazz station. At some point you made us a smoothie with mostly oranges. Fantastic. I had given Rae mixed signals about when I was coming over, she sent me confused emails, I assured her I'd be right over. She had to go to the bank. I printed the rest of the materials, hopped over to her place in the car. I was going to scooter over, but wanted to keep the papers flat. I saw Chuck there, said hello, Rae was waiting. I gave her the papers, we chatted about cancer a little bit, she asked if the diet was too strict, if I was too weak, if I was losing too much weight too fast. 25 lbs in three months sounds good to me. She was nice, we sat there and chatted. I had to go. I drove back home. You thought I'd been gone for two hours, it was 45 minutes. We had a little time before our information session about foster parenting. I can't remember what we did, it might have been Pilates or was that in the evening? I think it was then, during that time. We drove to foster parenting, a little hard to find, down in Mission Valley. I didn't know what it was about. They had a very particular mission and program, I would recommend it to anyone who wants to raise a child and meet parents in lots of trouble. I enjoyed it, there was one foster mother, Martha, who presented very well, funny, animated, sweet. They didn't discriminate against nontraditional couples. We were learning a lot. I looked at all the other couples and singles, all older than us, all wanting children aggressively. So many children, abused, neglected, beaten, burnt. I wanted to save them all, but could I even save one? 30% chance you keep the child, each time, same percent that I get deceased. It changed the chance. What if you were alone with this, would it be better? I'm not supposed to even think about it, but I did, I did. There were too many questions: These people already had four children, wanted more, to "grow their families." I don't know what we wanted. When we got home we talked about it, I didn't want to but we did. We found no resolution. I kept asking about our motives. Perhaps we should continue to discuss. We watched part of a documentary about Roger Ebert and verified that he was not a good man.

AUGUST 6, 2014

Yesterday yes all the little things:

Several orange butterflies flattering around the passion fruit plants on the fence. One brown one. Too many flies which cause stress.

The white part of Ronald's black muzzle beard in the sunshine.

One of those skinny girls who waddles, their legs never touch, they waddle on earth. Her overall shorts. Flip flops flapping. Big bun on her head, loose and brown but not falling. Sunglasses. Too happy too friendly lower voice.

Gabe at the pool reading a sci-fi book with light in the title, the book is silver and reflective, but I don't say this. A drunken girl in the pool with a pitcher of mojitos and a straw, the best on four continents. A floppy hat and a bikini, possibly mismatched, I can't remember.

A woman holding a baby in a sling too big to be a baby, it has real feet and hands.

Two young girls getting their picture taken, all flattered. Later one of the girls holds the too big baby, dancing, they all dance with the baby. Babies are good excuses for dancing.

A douchebag photographer in a red Hawaiian shirt blocks everyone's view, even the singer's.

A wood-slatted stool with no back that probably belonged to the skinny girl and a short plastic lattice green and white sort of French chair. A black wooden rocking chair no one sits in.

A blond child with scabs on his face grabs your butt.

Two other blond children spin around in puffy chairs. One has an Ikea backpack on the size of ours but it looks huge and orange on him.

A security guy who looks familiar in khakis with his legs too far apart like there's something big down there. There's nothing there. It's a ridiculous walk, uncomfortable for everyone involved.

Lots of people look familiar. The older taller woman with the short bleached hair and a short desert printed mini-dress with long sleeves. Her legs are tan. Her sunglasses are red. She keeps pulling her dress down. Her son is her son, blond and tan and chubby and wearing sneakers and jeans and a Brady Bunch kind of t-shirt. He is all Brady Bunch with severely side-parted sun bleached hair and shy. I might know them.

My light blue polka dotted shorts onesie from the 1930s with two buttons in the back. My high waisted orange bikini bottom and black and orange polka dotted bra top stays underneath.

Ashtanga primary series with my black knee brace on. Sun on the yoga mat. Small blue chips of yoga mat come up. One tiny non-biting ant on the mat gets it.

Baby Boston bibb lettuce and pickled red onion and blue cheese and a tiny pancetta crumble. Pancetta tastes too piggy. Potato soup with orange hot pepper oil and chilies. Roasted vegetables in chimichurri. I wipe off the table with my big cloth napkin when we're done. Crumbs.

We have no matches in the car but a serious Swiss army knife, a corkscrew, a first aid kit, a roll of blue window washing towels. You discover a plug outlet in the back seat.

Lots of people have eye masks on. Some poorly drawn in silver, some black netting, some strap-on cat masks. An older woman who looks like Suzanne's future with a big yellow bun in back, clipped in, wears a fringed Buddha jacket with tablecloth sleeves. Her crew takes her photo from behind over and over.

A young man wears a tight white dress and a blond wig. He can't walk, he can't hide his boy walk. Why when men dress like women do they try to act so respectable. Like the first thing about being a female is keeping it all tight. They can tell everyone is looking at them. Welcome.

A young woman faces us guarding the front section in a red security shirt and black pants. She is tall and wears a long black ponytail. Her face is pursed. She looks at everyone but doesn't want anyone looking at her. She is inside there.

I hold a man's hamburger for a second. I almost touch the bun.

Your ear bleeds in one tiny spot and I wipe it off. Did I get blood on the hamburger?

Poufy short dresses, lots of cocktail wear, high heels. One woman's are too big for her and she tries to keep them on by walking like a scared duck. A guy in a cartoon dinosaur suit.

The Good, the Bad and the Ugly. Who's who really? The big faces on screen are matched with distance shots of silhouettes. Black colored strangers and horses.

My buckwheat pillow is a beanbag. I have one eyelash growing downwards into my eye. It's white at the root. You help me push it up.

08.06.2014

Yesterday we slept. Yesterday we woke. Yesterday we found out that Spoon was playing for free at the pool at the Lafayette. Yesterday we ate eggs baked inside avocados. Yesterday we had a thin green juice. Yesterday we wrote our yesterdays. Yesterday we looked at our computers. Yesterday we talked about it, how we're not supposed to worry. Yesterday we ate our vitamins. Yesterday we read books. Yesterday we talked about it, will there be a child? Yesterday we went to the Lafayette, waited in line. Yesterday we saw Gabe there, he was talking to a girl. Yesterday we waited for the show, clearly acoustic, poolside. Yesterday among 200 people. Yesterday the show took forever to start. Yesterday we moved to the shade. Yesterday we decided maybe we'd go see Spoon and Arcade Fire and Dan Deacon and the amphitheater at the Amphitheatre. Yesterday we looked on Craigslist for decent tickets. Yesterday we found some, made plans with the guy. Yesterday there would be no tickets until six. Yesterday you made plans for our anniversary, officially starting today. Yesterday plans in Palm Springs, the Workshop and the Ace Hotel. Yesterday it sounded like shit once it started, at the pool. Yesterday it was just two dudes from the band, the singer and another utility guy. Yesterday they didn't know what to expect when they walked out. Yesterday the other guy's guitar and keyboard kept cutting out. Yesterday they sort of won everyone over anyway, won their own fans over. Yesterday everyone was wearing a bathing suit. Yesterday the sun was hot but there was a breeze. Yesterday Gabe told us about the CA bus pass, about how Tina and Grant were going to drive all the way down Baja, like we were always going to do. Yesterday Spoon sort of mailed it in. Yesterday we talked about that, about performing the same things everywhere. Yesterday

I thought a little about how I don't really like the things I liked ten years ago, Spoon, though the earlier stuff still has a little audacious minimalism that resonates with me in their pop/underground context. Yesterday I remembered there was no underground. Yesterday there was no ground. There was a shining pool, with people drinking daiquiris, putting one hand up. Yesterday we remembered why we hated radio stations. Yesterday 94.5 was plastered everywhere, one of their photographers in a Hawaiian shirt with his camera in the singer's face. Yesterday we rode our scooter home, walked the dogs, we exercised, one upstairs, one down. Yesterday we drank our orange and chocolate smoothies, we named our drink. Yesterday we looked on the internet for a restaurant with farms. Yesterday we decided on the Red Door, they get everything from their own organic garden. Yesterday we got dressed and went there. Yesterday we had happy hour, red wine and some delicious vegetables. Yesterday we texted the ticket seller. Yesterday he came to the restaurant, I walked out and gave him $, he handed me the tickets from his car. Yesterday I remembered buying drugs on the street, not in the store like I do now. Yesterday we finished our meal. Yesterday we drove to Chula Vista. Yesterday you bought the new Spoon record on iTunes, we played it in the car. Yesterday I remembered why I don't listen to Spoon anymore. Yesterday we got into the parking lot very easily. Yesterday the Amphitheatre was kind of incredible. Yesterday we looked for our great seats. Yesterday Spoon was already playing and it was still daylight. Yesterday they sounded better with their actual instruments, the new songs we hated sounded fine too. Yesterday we could see the occupation it was, the little gestures too small for that stage. Yesterday there was no one there at first. Yesterday we felt a little sorry for Spoon. Yesterday Dan Deacon came on. Yesterday I told you about Dan Deacon. Yesterday Dan Deacon played an amazing set, complete with dance instructions and genius declarations like, "Imagine you're in the middle of a giant amphitheater." Yesterday he made art. Yesterday his set was pretty short, we went to buy a record. Yesterday we looked around at this strange place, an overpriced village wrapped around a venue. Yesterday there were only 20 Yelps about this Amphitheatre. Yesterday we realized we had never heard of it before. Yesterday Arcade Fire started, the place was packed, the real show started. Yesterday we watched the first song. Yesterday the lights. Yesterday the fans with their fake black eyes. Yesterday we left, took the long road to our car. Yesterday we left before the headliner had finished their second song, the workers had to open the gate to let us out. Yesterday I set you down off a high wall. Yesterday we drove out among zero cars. Yesterday we learned about where the 805 goes. Yesterday we were sleepy when we got home. Yesterday we tried to force ourselves to get high but the Panda was clogged. Yesterday we watched the credits for *The Good, the Bad and the Ugly* and fell asleep.

FOUR

08.07.2014

Yesterday we spent, like, 600 dollars.

AUGUST 7, 2014

Yesterday was Ikea six words long.

08.08.2014

Yesterday woke up a little late, yesterday really went into the evening before, in the studio on our backs watching *The Good, the Bad and the Ugly* 'til two in the morning, you were mostly sleeping beside me, but I was into it, the music, the silence, the slowness. The tension. Each of the trilogy has a part where Clint gets tortured, this time the worst, the 100-mile hike through the desert, Tuco on his horse with his parasol. And I loved the way Clint was the good, though he was a killer, he simply had a little tinge of forgiveness. Lee Van Cleef was the bad, but was he the same character as in *For a Few Dollars More*? But we went to bed, slept, and woke up late. We had something to eat, I can't remember what, maybe I made oatmeal, that seems right. Lately I've been putting 1/2 steel cut oats, 1/4 chia seeds, 1/4 hemp seeds—it works well, and provides more nutrients. We had an appointment with the dermatologist, Brouha, in La Jolla at 11:30, and we had to head to the desert today, tomorrow—which meant we had to clean our house and set it up for our next renters. Also, I had to get more tenure materials together and drop them off at UCSD, so I printed some stuff off and made a stack. I grabbed some more of my old books as well. I drove us to the appointment and we got there just in time, parked in the underground lot but the elevator wouldn't come so we took the stairs, and that hurt your knee, so we were a few minutes late. This doctor is nice, but I don't know if he is helping. He tells us a lot about what he doesn't know, which makes for a pleasant exchange, but not too informative. We left and drove through La Jolla towards campus. I thought of the Angela Davis I'd been reading, how slavery and gender worked in La Jolla. I went into the poison lit building to run up to my office, grab my other materials and drop them off, but first

I checked to see if the academic files coordinator was in. She was. I can't believe there's a job for that. She tried to tell me what I needed: everything I've ever done, which seems excessive for someone with four books. But I said I'd try. It took me a while to label the things I had, and I knew you were in the car, suffering with no keys, no radio, no A/C. But I had to get this stuff in. The coordinator kept trying to tell me more when I went down to drop it off, but I kept telling her I had to run. She wouldn't listen. Finally I got away. You weren't happy, and I was sorry. We went to Ocean Beach to the co-op to get supplies, we bought vitamins and bottles for the compost and NuttZo and bags for future produce. We got so many things, we shared a little plate of organic food. That place is magic, we were healed. We drove home and started working on the house a bit. I made two beds, started cleaning the studio and the trailer. It was later in the day now. We needed to get more stuff, we need more stuff. I found that there was a new organic juice bar going in around the corner, we could walk by there and see if it existed yet, and then check out the new cheese shop in Bottlecraft. So we did that instead of work more, and this time we brought the dogs, who rarely get walked into town. The juice place was still under construction, but you went into the cheese place and I was going to bring the dogs in but there was a Great Dane in there so I went around the corner but when I came back the Great Dane was gone so I brought the dogs in and they were good. But you were worried, and I realized they could break all these beer bottles and I took them back out. The dogs behaved. We walked them back home and had some tiny slices of the cheese. We cleaned some more. I did my martial arts workout, stumbling around the basement. You made us dinner, polenta and some delicious mushrooms and salad from the farmer's market. Lovely, we ate dinner at 10. We cleaned a bit more, took the dogs out, got in bed and watched the rest of *Louie* season 4, the three last episodes where young Louie starts getting stoned and almost ruins his life and old Louie sees his twelve-year-old daughter smoking weed and we talked forever about how could we handle it if our kid was as bad as we were. Then the melatonin started buzzing in me, I had to sleep, and that's exactly what happened yesterday.

AUGUST 8, 2014

Yesterday we saw an old dermatologist who looks young. Last time he was wearing Chucks, this time a suit, I think purple. Lavender. Is the care of the patient dependent upon the relative attractiveness of the wife.

I can't walk up the steps, two flights, but do it anyway, slowly. If something feels bad it must be good for your knee. We walk down, I use you as an escalator. We walk up two more flights at the co-op, then down. I wonder if people think I'm old this way. They have glass baby bottles and pullover bajas there, pretty much everything you'd need. We get two glass bottles for our oils and three mesh produce bags.

You go into the cancer building to put together the file. You forgot your little round yellow stickers at home. You're in there for almost an hour, I wait in the car without keys in the sun. I get pissed. We discuss.

Yesterday we walked the dogs into public. Up to the juice job not yet open, all plywood report, all windows with brown paper. It's hard to believe the juice will be there, next to the butcher and the butt shop.

We walk down 30th to Bottlecraft. I go in to buy Venissimo cheeses. I taste a gouda from Holland and a white truffle from Italy. I get small cuts of both. I ask if the cheeses are all grass-fed, have all these cheeses fed on grass? She says something about Europe and a co-op. I'm one of those people is another phrase.

You walk into the shop with both dogs, all three of you look quite proud. All I can think of is all those brown beer bottles breaking to the floor when the dogs freak out. I buy a local chocolate bar for the guests, with nuts. We taste the cheeses at home.

We clean for a few hours. The restaurant with the three-course vegetarian meal closes at 10 but we decide not to go. I make polenta and mushrooms and tomatoes. I think I use too much oil. We have some more cheese on our salad. The mushrooms are meaty.

We watch three *Louie*'s. We stay up late talking about how to prevent a drug-addicted overdosing child. Obviously there's nothing. I think you might want to procreate rather than borrow or rent-to-own someone else's. I like the pregnancy idea for the foods, mostly. Also the look. I like seeing pregnant women in the aisles of the hippie co-op. Yesterday I saw three. Everyone else had clearly adopted.

We share a plate of fennel salad and hemp seed tabbouleh, quinoa and I think some rice thing. A cup of straight up green tea. A woman sits down near us and looks at me with recognition. That's all I can say about it. Everyone eating on the patio is a woman. Except you, you look dashing in your full wide red beard, also sad.

In the dark we talk about our childhoods and clearly I've got the hangup. You have your useful creation myths. You tell me a general memory of helping your dad in the garage building things, his assistant, how much time you spent with him. I think you might be glossing over some bad shit, but I don't say that. I tell you a specific memory about my parents meeting me when I was late for curfew and my father going into gory detail about how nice it was that he could tell my mother was a virgin when he married her.

My memory is an emblem, yours is a flag.

I almost have a panic attack going to sleep knowing that I'm insane and will become only more so, especially with an imaginary child and you so unphasable. Then I realize I'll probably be fine, chin up chest out and that.

At some point yesterday, I decided to be less of an asshole if possible. There's really no reason to be such a dick.

08.09.2014

Yesterday we had to finish getting the house ready to rent it to Delphine, from France. We'd saved quite a bit to do, and wanted to get to the desert place in time to get to Pappy and Harriet's before the show. We are a machine on these days, we have our allotted tasks and our expectations for each other's performance. I started by loading the car, putting the old wooden office chair in the back on its side, then carefully placing items we'd packed around it where they hopefully wouldn't break. We had Ikea stuff for the new house, food for us and the dogs, our clothing (a little less than usual this time, as we're getting our washing machine delivered soon). We worked a while then walked to the Mission for breakfast. It is said they get their produce and eggs locally, so we went for it, both for the indulgence and the ease, especially to avoid messing up the kitchen. I almost threw a rock into a pickup when we were trying to cross the crosswalk, the one with flashing lights clearly marked that no one ever stops for, when we tried to cross and the tough guy practically ran us down. I believe in a society that stops for pedestrians, I believe that the key to a neighborhood is being able to cross busy streets where it is so marked, I believe in order, I suppose. I yelled angrily, loudly, but he didn't notice. I was enraged but calmed down quickly, I didn't want you to see it, or to see me pummeled in the street. It was a delicious pile of food, you ordered the hippie breakfast or whatever it is called, the one with tofu and brown rice. I had the potatoes stacked high with jalapeños and gluten-free bread. We knew we'd be eating out a bit today, and tried to use restraint. The restaurant was packed but we got our table quickly and enjoyed sitting there amidst the noise. We had had that waiter before, and he showed a little recognition, maybe we joked a bit. We had a conversation of some kind, maybe about the neighborhood, how this place was one of the first flags of gentrification, then we heard "White Rabbit" on the stereo and we talked about drugs and revolution, about commodification, then we talked about babies. We walked back home, easier crossing University this time, back to the house where we had more cleaning and preparation to do. I took care of the outside, wiping off the chairs, sweeping, and raking. I picked up the big bag of dog poop, some poop juice ran down the bag onto my hand when I passed it over the fence onto the top of the garbage can, totally disgusting. I washed it off in the outdoor shower, but couldn't get the scent out of my nose. We kept working, I made our bed for the strangers, moved all kinds of stuff into the basement, vacuumed the house and mopped it. You did your things, everything else. Things looked good. It was 2:30 and I took the dogs out to the car so you could put the finishing touches on it. The dogs were so excited to go on a trip, overwhelming enthusiasm. We sat in the driveway, and Ronald barked fiercely at a kid in a wheelchair coming by. I pinched his neck, hard, told him never never, Kiki crouched in fear. We drove the path we've memorized to Landers, but with a little detour you found on your phone that got us out of some traffic. We listened to Courtney Barnett on the phone. We weren't that impressed, the references were too easy, too much piano plucking. You found the Bills game on the radio, on your phone. You were playing the phone like a maestro. We pulled over and I got some of the popcorn and trail mix out of the back of the car. The Bills played better this week, it sounded like. We made it to Landers, the house as lovely as ever, clean from last time, and we still had a few hours to hang out, which we did. The dogs ran around, Kiki lost her little light. It wasn't that hot in the desert. We drove to Pappy's to check out Courtney Barnett and hopefully get a table. They sat us right away. It was a miracle. We had had this waitress before, there was no recognition, but we were in front of the TV that shows the band and I watched them set up, you had your back to them and I could tell from their Teiscos they would at least be interesting. I played gear snob. We shared the salmon and the kale salad and two sides of vegetables. We had a glass of wine each. The first band was called Crystal Skulls, which is a terrible name, but I thought they were maybe a little brilliant in their way. The psychedelic non-dangerous beach rock thing, but with cool changes and good singing. Must have been from LA. We were getting happy in our retreat environment, and our food was good and healthy. You sat next to me for a while and watched the band and we were people who were impressed. We paid, went to the car and smoked a one-hitter, breathed the pot and the night desert air. I thought Courtney Barnett had a lot of buzz, but that's the thing about Pappy's, you can be front row to things you could never approach at home. I would like to break down the show we saw here, but will keep it quick: the band was great, proficient, crafty, tight, and they were having fun. The music was completely derivative, but for me, 20 years older than the star, in a sweet spot. In college when she was born, listening to the music she was copying, copying with talent and ingenuity, but copying. She's known for her lyrics, I'd read it's a combination of Dylan, Nirvana, and Kimya Dawson, but of course that's too much. You were in front of me and I could feel you doing your thing, evaluating the performance, what was real, what was forced, what was driven by gender, and you were right, it's just an impossible thing to be a woman on a stage, but I thought it was a sincere deal, perhaps missing a bit of edge because there is no edge anymore, perhaps a bit giddy, a little babyish, but she played her guitar barehanded and she has smart lyrics and the people were into it, old and young, male and female, white and tan from the desert sun. We were near the bass player and I missed playing my bass, made a note to do just that, sometime, real loud, with someone on drums, hopefully you. She apologized for not writing more songs because she would like to play them for this little audience, then she played a song alone, a song about looking at a house for sale in Australia, something about if she had a half million she could tear it down. Nothing changed but it was a good night, and we drove home through the stars and on the radio was the immortal Jimi Hendrix.

AUGUST 9, 2014

Yesterday just the plot:

Woke up in a round bed.

Made a pot of sencha green tea. Bag not leaf. White Swedish teapot.

Cleaned and re-cleaned the house for the French guests. Sprayed and wiped surfaces.

Ronald and Kiki too excited. Put them out or leave them in. Left them in. Put them out.

Went to the Mission for breakfast. I had the zen with tofu, zucchini, squash, brown rice, egg whites. You had the papas with soy chorizo, avocado, scrambled eggs, rosemary bread. Hot sauces. We shared a fresh squeezed orange juice.

We had to walk slow.

A small blond boy on the corner with three unidentified adults entertains himself obnoxiously. Runs in circles and is too happy.

I wear my X t-shirt. I pack eye shadow for the desert. I find a cream shadow I forgot about. It's red. I put it on my eyes.

We clean some more. It takes hours. I pack up the fridge into a cold bag with no ice packs. I use frozen vegetables and berries. You take the last swig of aloe juice.

I leave a ribbon and a note on a bottle of California wine. I leave Calabria coffee and jars of tea. I leave notes. I leave a note about lighting the stove. I leave bottles of water and glasses in the bedrooms. I fold towels and place soaps on top. I place the rugs. I lint roll the pillows and cushions. I wipe down the baseboards and the light switches and the door handles. I wash out the fridge. I clean off the washer and dryer. I wash more dishes. I put away dishes. I put slippers in the pockets of the robes.

You sweep out back, you pack the car, you get the wood chair in there. You rake the yard, you scoop all the dog poo and put out a new bag in the can. You sweep up spider webs. You vacuum everything and mop and make up the round bed. You hang the robes where I can't reach. You get down a lot of things I can't reach. You put up things I can't reach.

I leave lights on. I leave the jazz station on the radio. I lock the door and the gate.

You drive us to get diesel then you drive us to the desert. I look at my phone. We get a text from Kiik. You get a text from Brett. We sit in traffic on the 15. My phone finds a better way and reroutes us through the back hills of suburban Temecula, past empty plots and cul-de-sacs with no houses and new houses. We pull over on a wide street and you get the chia seed popcorn and trail mix from the back. We drink water. I give the dogs our water. Kiki gazes at you while you drive. Ronald sticks his head out the window. We don't stop.

We see a sign in Morongo that says organic Medjool dates. I ask if palm trees were always here or were they imported from somewhere, why Medjool, Spain?

We get to the desert house. It is white and cool and the outside lights are on. I unlock the gate. Ronald and Kiki go running. You turn on the water pump and the hot water heater. You give them water out back, I give them water inside. I feed them. I unpack all the foods—mushrooms, peppers, zucchini, oranges, apples, lemons, onions, nuts, goji berries, muesli. You unload everything from the car.

We lie in the hammocks out back, one red and one blue. The sun sets. The dogs run. Kiki loses her light somewhere.

I drive us to Pappy's. We get a table in front of the screen behind the sound guy. We order the kale salad and salmon with two veggies, broccoli and parsnips-carrots. You get a Cab and I get a Malbec. We each drink two cups of water.

I look at all the outfits. A couple in silk patterned jackets, an older blond in a side ponytail and a black Bad Brains t-shirt, an anorexic in a long denim shirt, three young girls in onesies, one in a tie-dyed dress, several peasant shirts, some pretty good leather. Ted Quinn. I look at all the hair and look out for a good mid-length or shorter cut.

We watch Crystal Skulls while we eat. You watch the screen. I keep my back to the screen and listen. The Smiths and the zeitgeist and pretty good. Then I sit next to you and we both watch the screen and a slit of stage. You put your arm around me. You pee. Then I pee.

We hit a one-hitter.

We watch Courtney Barnett and the Courtney Barnetts standing up, then sitting down, then standing up again. Courtney Barnett is a big guitar playing baby. She baby-mouths the microphone like a bottle. She has a heart-shaped head. She wears my clothes from 1992 when I wasn't allowed in family pictures. I tell you this later.

You drive us home and I look out the skylight. You watch for mice trying to die in the road.

08.10.2014

Yesterday was a long day. What does that mean? There was a full moon later, into today, I suppose, and I'm not sure if we heard the coyotes today or yesterday, but we heard them and it seemed like there was a human party going on. Earlier we had run some errands around the town, the rows of strip malls like insipid brown Legos. We had a big-box/little-box consumer sandwich going on, Home Depot, the farmer's market, Sue's Health Foods, the appliance store to confirm our delivery. There, the woman told us they had a set to match the oven we bought. She showed it to us and it was a wall of ovens, beautiful top-of-the-line '80s appliance with push buttons and dials like some kind of HAL. But then we would have three ovens for two of us in the desert, and we don't make roasts. I kind of still want it, and I know you do, you don't want to break the set, but there's no need for it at all. I hadn't slept well the night before and we slept a bit yesterday through the day. It was a long day, which is good sometimes, we looked at the stars for a while at the end of the day and the dogs were free to roam as much as they wanted, though for the most part they stayed with us. We had the A/C on earlier, but when I exercised and made dinner we left it on, turned it off in the earlier evening and let the hot-cooling breeze in. We got plenty of veggies, and plenty of tools at Home Depot. Home Depot is like no depot I've ever seen, it's more like a museum of facts that you need to understand how to use. How do they decide where to send you when you walk in, like in the evil groceries you're shot straight towards the potato chips and corn-syrup sodas. In Home Depot there are two entrances on either side of the place, two exits as well, and then there's also a contractor's entrance as well. Then there's a small door for tool rentals. I suppose you might walk into the ceiling fans, but everything is specialized. I was looking for a screwdriver, a small one to put together an Ikea picture frame, and a chihuahua almost attacked me from his foxhole in his owner's cart. We couldn't find the bathroom in there. We only ate small snacks all day until I made some stuffed peppers for dinner, filled with quinoa and covered with a quick red sauce. Here's how to do it: carmelize some cut tomatoes in oil on an iron pan, along with whole cloves of garlic, then transfer them into the oven for 20 minutes or so. Then blend in your Vitamix. It makes a good, no fuss sauce. We visited the Panda out front, the dogs do whatever we say when we are stoned. We tried to watch *The Grand Duel* from our Spaghetti Western DVD but my MacBook died after 20 minutes, the cord we brought doesn't work with it. I had this other laptop, the one I'm typing on now, the Sony. I thought it was a terrible thing, but it is useful, it plays DVDs, so we tried that after we did it sweetly. There is a UFO convention in town and when we sat outside again, we thought we saw something moving, but it's all basically satellites. I'd like to describe our desert home for those of you who are reading this, but this project is about what happened, not what it looks like. You are all invited to a big party sometime soon. I thought a little about how the desert seems so good, how you and I are now ordained, how we will marry our friends together in the desert in a month. It agrees with us. I did this workout where you jump a thousand times, I could feel the oxygen attacking all the inflammation from the surgery. There were no UFOs or bats, not even my soul creature the white owl, who flew out of a tree when I sat on the bench below him. Which brings us to the last thing we watched, the documentary on Leonard Cohen taming the mob audience at the Glastonbury Fest in 1970. I had no idea. 600,000 people were there for five days. They were lighting the stage on fire, burning the gates and walls. They were knee-deep in trash. Hendrix and The Who played, Kris Kristofferson was booed off the stage. The youth were restless and pointless. Leonard Cohen came on at 4 in the morning and his performance was presented as calming the mob. The footage was fantastic. His band was called The Army. Have you ever heard the early songs of Leonard Cohen? It's complete Canadian Dylan, but with songs that build, songs that are willing to go completely melodramatic, songs with desperation. Ok, the guy was a genius but the reason there wasn't a riot was because the kids were sleepy and high and they wanted to listen to the poetry, which was substantial. They wanted someone to look them straight in the eye and make them feel stupid.

AUGUST 10, 2014

Yesterday Leonard Cohen took us down, by the river, where we could hear the British chatter, we could go on this way forever...

They say he stepped out of his trailer in pajamas. I wanted to see that part. Instead he held crowd in a safari suit almost skirt-like, mop head almost Dylan, almost Prince Valiant. You just have to believe there were almost riots.

Leonard Cohen does what both poetry and music do, but also what French does: delayed syntax, orchestrated image, nasal intonation, repetitive upswing from low tone, mood over melody. Leonard Cohen does it best at 4 in the morning.

We decided not to focus only on Leonard from yesterday.

We also went to the desert farmer's market in Joshua Tree where the people and the vegetables looked like they'd been better. You saw the Joshua Tree Sherriff walking through, she was waving like in a parade but just walking in her Sherriff suit. You pointed her out to me, how did you know she was the for real Sherriff, I thought she was just an old lady doing something crazy.

We went back to Carlos' Appliances to arrange the delivery. Our new used appliances were marked "sold." Carlos was out but his wife was in. She showed us the matching wall ovens we could get. We would have three ovens then, what does anyone do with three ovens. Families, another problem.

She showed us something that blew her mind, a whole house water filtration system. It looked like a helium tank for balloons or scuba. I told her she should keep it, it's good for your hair and skin. She said they get reports on the contaminations in the water in 29 Palms, not good.

We got a bag of peppers from the market, I wasn't sure how we'd eat them all. I said casually, maybe we could stuff them. I've never stuffed a pepper, I don't know what I'm talking about. Then all of a sudden, you're stuffing peppers and making them. Three peppers, red and green, with quinoa, zucchini, mushrooms, and a roasted tomato and garlic puree on top. Plus a little bit of that gouda and truffle cheese from Venissimo, the last of it. I'm glad it's gone.

Is this boring or is this a record. Is a record boring. Is it playing with boredom. Is it evidence that we are not the same body after all. You get cancer, I don't. We have our own days. Did I say that before?

New thought: the monument of yesterday is hilarious, as if something really happened. And if it did, it would already be over. It all sounds so grave, so equally significant.

I wore a little cotton shirt I almost gave away with small yellow and brown and blue cornflowers drawn on it, a ruching around the cap sleeves and a linen panel at the top. It's a very girly shirt and I look like a girl in it. Especially with my dirty hair in a bun. I wear cut off jean shorts and a nice little sprinkle of leg hair.

I am always moving from past to present tense like a downhill, I just can't quit the present. Is this wrapping up or will it go on forever? How is a Leonard Cohen song about a woman also about a city? Why are women and children still one category?

We look for Kiki's light but it's lost. We walk on the sand in our desert yard, or is it a compound, or a rancho, or an estate. A grounds.

Nothing really happened yesterday. I looked at my pink iPhone a little bit. Delphine had a question about where to get groceries when they got in. I answered her an hour later, is that too late. Rae had a question about your book. I typed her back because your fingers are too big to type on a phone.

I bought us two bags of kale chips at Sue's Foods. I made fun of going to Sue's Foods, all one word, slurring. We ate the kale chips all over ourselves, all over the car, all over our teeth.

I dropped my electric toothbrush on the ground and it broke. That might have been the day before.

We need to spend more time outside here.

08.11.2014

Yesterday I was thinking about Westerns, specifically about the Spaghetti
version, but also about the other varieties: the Classic Western, the Space
Western, and, for lack of a better name, the Postmodern Western. I've never
read anything anyone has to say about these things, not because I'm not
interested, but because I wouldn't know where to begin. But it seems to me
that all of these varieties revolve around a kind of nostalgia for a lapsed
kind of homosocial masculinity that is wedded to the concept of open space
and frontier. Many of these (and I'm talking about movies here) feature a
trio of men who are ambiguous in terms of ethics, but their feelings about
justice and the way they value life is revealed through the course of the
film. One becomes the villian, though he has reasons. One is young and
virile. One is older but badass. It's the good the bad and the ugly, but that
updates the paradigm, because all are killers. It's more Luke, Darth Vader,
and Obi-Wan, but that film is made for a trilogy, so there's also Han, who
also has a complex sense of frontier justice — probably tossed in because the
Jedi and the Empire were too simply possessed of a ethos. They even added
Chewbacca, who's kind of a monster, as a sidekick. It's Jimmy Stewart,
John Wayne, and Liberty Valance. Who wants to put up fences, to inscribe
order on the plains, on the desert, on outer space itself, and who wants to
murder freely, to rape and take whatever there is to grab? Bags of coin, gold
from the ground, bounties, a railroad right through a new town. The films
are very satisfying, because their conventions are so apparent, and because
any fudging with the generic borders seems radical. I wonder how many
Westerns were made — there is always another one, and every male movie
star before the '70s except for Cary Grant had an entire career in them.

Even Joel McCrea, even Jimmy Stewart—no John Wayne types there—learned to ride horses and draw guns. And what's up with the guns? The fastest draw, the feats of pyrotechnic aim, the shot that makes the hat spin into the dusty wind—every film is made of these shots, of these examples of perfect control of chaos. I guess the main reason they made so many was, of course, because people bought tickets for them, but also because the desert light was so intense they were able to shoot without expensive lighting, and also because the settings were so spectacular that often the action was more a way to provide a background. But more interesting are the moments that the "civilized" world weighs in, when the Civil War shows up, way out here in California or Oklahoma, where soldiers become bounty hunters or keep their beefs long after the war is over. It's the reason so many of them can shoot, the reason so many want to be as far away from people as possible. And sometimes there are black characters, some of whom wear their slave past in their eyes and shoulders but are now riding alongside the heroes or villains. And sometimes the later versions, or the Italian ones, promote a black character or a Native American character, or a female character above the average white maleness to a position where there is some power. Not all the way (though I still have many to see) but further. The contemporary struggles are revealed askance. But generally, Westerns are just super-racist, especially anything before the sixties. Then there is the violence, the ingenious places bullets can enter the body, the camera showing us a mountain through a man's chest. I didn't really have a thesis yesterday, I was just thinking about Westerns. I was thinking about how we got this place out here that looks exactly like the movies we watch, and how we should shoot our own Westerns. I would write Leonard Cohen-ish songs for the score, and we could act like two poets sharing our adventures out here in the frontier. We could start a web series, if we really applied ourselves, I imagine people would watch it. People will watch anything, for instance Westerns. One thing's for sure, kids die often in these movies—there is no better way to earn proper rage for revenge. You woke up yesterday and told me you'd been up thinking the night before, between reading the Bill Bryson book one of our guests left at our house and Angela Davis, the night before you were thinking maybe we should have our own baby rather than adopt—there was so much more freedom there—and I agreed wholeheartedly, though all my life I have sworn never to add to the problem called society.

AUGUST 11, 2014

Yesterday is getting harder to remember.

I couldn't sleep from 2-6 so I finally turned on the light and read Angela Davis. You had your sleep mask on, you slept.

Angela Davis' middle name is Yvonne. She laments the lack of texts on women and slavery while she is writing one. This Angela Davis book is an old yellowed paperback with a personal embossed stamp from Eloise Klein Healey in it. I don't know how we ended up with this copy of this book. I hallucinate that the margin marks are mine, especially the stars. But when I read the cursive, it's not mine. I remember this book from one of my women's studies classes, from my women's studies major at UW. Race and Class are the intersections at UW, whereas I remember Buckley telling me that Religion was the intersection at UC-Boulder. The book is dedicated to her mother, Sallye, Angela Yvonne's. Davis details the lives of women under slavery and the difference in the place of work in the lives of white women and black women. I've read this book before but you recently got it out of the studio after we had an argument and I said you needed a re-education. You've never read this book before. You started reading it one night and couldn't put it down. You were shocked and horrified by the facts. A lot of the book at the beginning is recounting and theorizing the family structure under slavery. Women are forced to leave their babies at the end of a row of cotton and pick, or else they must pick with their babies on their back. I remember you telling me about this part and as I read, the facts unfold in reverse of how you told them and how I just told them now. Facts unfold in reverse and the story is told in a way the teller and the receiver can process. This is why there's so much of the story we never know. We can never be the story. I like the way she italicizes *rape*. *Rape* as the one element distinguishing women's slave lives from men's. It's totally fucked up to say I like that, I mean, that she italicizes it, but it's a pretty fucking important point. It's also important, I find, to use rape in italics in an argument with a man who doesn't fucking get shit, to ask him if he has ever feared *rape*, ever walked home in the middle of the street, rather get hit by flying cars than followed, grabbed, raped, which is almost inevitable. But I do wonder if the male slave owners didn't also rape the men, if that's a story, because are women really just that much easier to rape than men. Under slavery isn't everyone raped. And if not why not. Are these questions too fucked up to ask. I don't put question marks in, as one copyeditor pointed out recently, well, not pointed out, but rather indexed, pointed, accused. That should be a question mark, she said. No, no it shouldn't be. Why. Period. I thought about this, this thought was inside my transcribing yesterday from my notebook parts of what might be part of that book that she incorrectly copyedited. I like that Angela Y. Davis' writing is academic for readables. She is just the facts, just the thoughts, just the things that need to be said, remembered, read in the middle of the night.

Then I read a little bit of this strange book that some guest at our house left inside my office cabinet. I found it in there when I was stashing things away from the next guest. I put the pot in there and I found this book in a spot I didn't think the guests would think to go, where I was hiding the pot. It's *A Walk in the Woods* by Bill Bryson, who sounds familiar. It's about him walking the Appalachian Trail, which he abbreviates as the AT. I guess he's some kind of popular travel writer, I keep thinking Robert Bly. His photo is on the back and he's white and sort of blond and scruffy and very chubby. It says he lived in England for ten years and you can hear it in his writing.

He's supposed to be very humorous. I'll admit the pages were almost as easy to turn as Angela's. But I think he's trying to be entertaining, rather than strictly factual or theoretical or groundbreaking or important. He's trying to be British in a very American way. He mentions his wife exactly twice. Once to say, My wife scowled. The other time to say, My wife frowned. Or something. She is an appendage to the kitchen. She is the airport ride. She is the judgmental overseer of children. Bly Bryson actually proves exactly what Angela Davis is theorizing, the straight white male patriarchal order that can't see anything outside its frame, pasting motherhood onto women when it serves them, denying motherhood and stealing children from mothers when the mothers and children serve them.

When you wake up I tell you I've been thinking very clearly. That we should have a baby instead of trying to save $30,000 to adopt one that already has a waiting list or rent-to-own a free one with a 30% chance of not getting to keep it. I tell you I remember what you said after the foster orientation, when you said, Why do we think that 30% is a good chance to get a baby, but 30% is a bad chance for my cancer to come back. Our lives are based on percentages. One more human on the planet is not incredibly irresponsible. One more white human is a question, but it might be responsible to make one more white ally, one more non-racist non-fascist human, if possible. You are very happy with this news. I want to read more Angela Y. Davis, I want us to.

08.12.2014

Yesterday was the day that we met a person. She had a hot tub that her grandmother had handed down to her at her wedding, and it had sat on her back porch for three years and now she had a baby and she wanted it cleared out. She was selling it real cheap, 175 dollars, and we found her on Craigslist. I think it was around noon or one o'clock. Previously we had eaten a smoothie and, I believe, some leftover rice and beans. I almost wrote rhythm and blues. Do I only know two songs that repeat yesterday prominently, The Beatles and The Cure? The woman lived in Yucca Valley and her puppy had chewed on the side of the hot tub. It was enormous. It takes 20 minutes to get to Yucca from our place. Each corner was missing wooden slats that covered the tub guts. But the rest looked clean, very clean, except for the dusty top, which was very nice actually, under the grime, and underneath, which was filled with detritus. I could tell you wanted it. The woman was young, but she had a baby, and her husband had told her they couldn't afford the $400 to hook the tub up. I could tell I wanted it. Too good of a deal, too great for our place in the desert, under the deep skies, soaking in warm water, listening to the coyotes cry. We went and got her money and then it occcured to me that we would need some muscle to move it. I only know one person out here — it's kind of the point, loneliness — and I'd only met him, Scott, once. But I knew he was attached to the worker underbelly of this depressed desert economy. I left him a message, he called right back. He could help tomorrow, he had a truck and a trailer, maybe he knew a few guys. The woman who sold it to us was nice, she sent me a text that said she had posted on Facebook that she needed some guys to help move a hot tub and that there would be five of them tomorrow at 3.

It only took an hour to round them up. I think they were all religious. I was organizing a tub moving. Well, she did most of it, but we don't have the internet out here. Yesterday I worked out in the morning and then we did yoga at night, or maybe that was the day earlier. Yesterday we had salad for dinner and I read *Malone Dies* for a while before we slept.

AUGUST 12, 2014

Yesterday was a Monday. Another Mondane as Courtney Barnett says, I think. Yesterday my hair looked like Prince Valiant, I looked like a prince. Why do princes always wear their hair like that, chopped between the chin and the shoulder. I can't remember anything about the morning, but there was tea, a gunpowder green leaf from the co-op you brewed in the black cold press, I think. I think there was a smoothie with berries and a nectarine, or maybe it was green, I can't remember. I think yesterday is the day Robin Williams killed himself and we started bombing Iraq again and I don't know what's happening in Palestine but obviously 1,000 Palestinians are worth 1 Israeli and this is the math we inherited from the 20th century, new maths. Maybe Ebola is creeping or maybe Ebola is cured because it hit an American. Maybe Canadians aren't as good as they used to be and Quakers too, if they ever were. We had our appliances brought over by Carlos and his guy, two old men carrying our new old fridge into the house and taking the old old one out. They were bummed how far away our house was, how many dirt roads they had to take to get to us. You gave them an extra $40 because we felt bad about that, they took the wrong road. Carlos told his guy to tell us we can have the washing machine hoses for free when we come into the store. He'll give us a special deal on the matching white glass wall ovens, three ovens. We had to buy some things so we went out. Sue's Foods was shit. We had to go to Vons to get toilet paper. A special trip for tp, that's always fun. I got us two avocados from the organics section. I got a hula hoop from the Angels thrift store next door. A hoop for every house. I didn't test it out. It's a very light hoop, hard to hula. I did yoga again with a knee brace on in the dark in the evening with only the swag lamp over the plywood table and the solar string bird lights on the wall. These yesterday reports don't include: current world events not involving us, shitting, dental hygiene, and fucking. The yesterday before yesterday I cut my hair, just grabbed two chunks and cut. You liked it. I'm going to keep going. Oh, p.s., yesterday we bought a used hot tub from some Christians. On the drive there, a raggedy tanned desert dude carrying a Mountain Dew crossed in front of us. I said, I wonder if he has an amazing singing voice, really just gorgeous.

08.13.2014

Yesterday there was a morning, an afternoon, an evening, and a night. Two a's and two an's. I woke early, or maybe didn't sleep well at all—the sun pours in through the blinds everywhere at 6. I've been trying to remember the sleep mask, it helps, you're absolutely right, but I don't like to put it on until I am done with my nocturnal activities, reading or watching Spaghetti Westerns on a laptop. When I put it on at the last minute, right before slipping out, the effort to grab it and place it over my eyes gets my blood roiling again, wakes me all over again. And the melatonin helps, but only to a degree, so I can pass out, but I can't go down consciously. The best technique is to wear the mask on my head like a bandanna and then drop it down at the last second. But I don't always have the foresight to do so. And I can't always find the mask. Also, it's either too loose or too tight, and I'm not terribly used to it, so if I wake with it on my face, I feel someone is trying to asphyxiate me through the eyes. It went like this: 6am: wake, look at my books, especially the book about concrete countertops. I learned a Chinese philosophical term that means a kind of architectual simplicity, I can't remember what it was. I looked at my Buddhism book, and learned a term for suffering, but the good kind, or, I guess value judgments are beside the point in these matters, I can't remember what it was, it started with a D. I wasn't really paying attention, I was just ambiently reading. I let K out because she wakes up like me, she wants to be in sun as soon as it's there to be had. I took my laptop outside, to the deck, and played one of my workout DVDs and tried to keep up. It was called Decelerator. The idea is that the body does something special when it lands from a jump or any kind of coiled manuever. I don't know, but the view we've purchased out here is something I never thought I could lay claim to, it goes far: mountains everywhere, boulders, skies. There was a morning breeze and some rain in it, too. It seems I did a lot yesterday, I should skip ahead. I want to talk about routines somewhere today, things that always happen, or happen so regularly that I forget to mention them. But first more about the day: you woke up slowly, took off your sleep mask. I had already begun making the oat/chia/ hemp–seed meal. I used the pressure cooker this time — less time, more skill involved. I left a burner on afterward, and felt terrible about it. I don't want to burn a baby. We ate. This is going too slow. I could make a list: a.) oatmeal, b.) berry smoothie, c.) nuts, d.) lovely dinner at the 29 Palms Inn. Or, a.) took off the moldings around the house that were too high from when I removed the carpets, b.) painted them white in the rain and sun, c.) nailed them back in lower, this time with clear caulk everywhere so as to keep the bugs out, d.) hooked up the water hose to the incredible refrigerator that shoots drinking water and ice out the front, e.) drove to Yucca Valley to put together my crack team of jacuzzi movers, meeting Scott there a little early, calling the owner, taking a pricker out of her dog's foot, chatting with strangers, watching large late Christians arrive slowly, trying to make self-deprecating small talk, thanking the husband for coming to help, realizing it was his house and making a joke, calling myself weak and friendless, just the pure performance of stranger anxiety, noticing the ragtag desert bunch of lifters: the husband in his "I Love My Wife" church T-shirt, the guy in the Raiders shirt and goatee, the huge marine who plays guitar in Scott's church band, the Raiders guy's son, who is going to Chico State in two weeks and who doesn't want to buy new construction boots anytime soon, guiding Scott and his truck and trailer as close as we could get to the monstrous jacuzzi, assembling everyone around it and lifting 'til I saw stars, the thing was so incredibly heavy, I felt like I wasn't doing anything, but when I stopped doing anything, the thing would fall to the ground, it must have weighed 1,000 pounds, or at least 500 as Scott said later, lifting and stumbling 'til we got it, miraculously to the trailer, and these guys were thrilled that they did it, that we did it, and I felt like I was in a Christian fraternity, I wanted to slap high fives, but they weren't ready yet, so I made a joke about coming up to Landers and helping unload the thing, because Scott and I would really have no chance of getting it off the trailer ourselves, we would die, we were the two tall skinny guys as you said later, and these other dudes were brutes and they had Jesus, well, Scott had Jesus too, everyone did but me, "Jesus Is Just Alright With Me," I heard that one on the radio earlier, Tom Petty's "Buried Treasure," which is a great radio show actually, we kept it on for the last few days, I've really learned a lot, like the fact that Jimmy Page and Jeff Beck were both in the Yardbirds at the same time for a few tracks, but the Christian fraternity was so nice, they all followed Scott and his slow hauling truck to our place and I followed them, they needed to complete the job, I saw that you had texted me because the electrician had finally showed up at our place, and we were all worrried that you might get raped but you didn't you just got condescended to mightily the way women and city folk are by old electricians, but it was ok to put the jacuzzi at our pad which was good news and we drove it and lifted it to the right spot on the pad and then I felt everyone was my friend, they were impressed with our place, so was I, it is the most beautiful place in the world, I don't want to die anytime soon, but sprinkle my dust out here if you read this, f.) hung out with Scott a bit and heard about his misadventures driving back from Oaxaca, g.) headed to another town to check it out, because they have an organic garden, h.) listened to the news about Robin Williams hanging himself from his closet door, also slitting his wrists, the coke and the self-medication, kind of felt it, you know, Robin Williams' mania, the always performing, heard on the embarrasingly predictable Lawrence O'Donnell show, heard Robin Williams talking about suicide with that one comedian who I want to be friends with whose voice is just like Mark Wallace's, Mark Maron I think, talked about it with you, told you about another story I heard on the radio earlier, when I was driving behind Scott and my brothers, on Progress radio, about the guy on the show seeing Robin Williams years ago, spotting Robin Williams in a bookstore and pointing him out to his girlfriend at the time, and how Robin Williams saw them looking and crumbled into his book in complete despair, and I felt guilty because we were bombing Iraq again, and the ceasefire was over, and the poor were getting poorer, and all I could think about was fucking Robin Williams who, sure, was at a bit of a career juncture, and sure was maybe always mentally ill, but then I told myself it's not good for me to feel guilty, cancer can grow in me if I think the wrong things, feel the wrong way, and I changed the channel to one playing "Hells Bells" and I cranked it but I had forgotten about your headache and I turned it down and tried to feel appropriately, safely, guilty for not being considerate, and i.) arrived at the 29 Palms Inn and had a lovely light dinner next to a pool listening to two musicians sounding kind of incredible with their casio keyboard and a muted trumpet playing jazz standards, and j.) watched a young foreign couple take their baby in the pool, and k.) ate the portabella, and l.) watched the couple return from the room with their baby and sit near us, I picked up the bottle the baby threw, flirted with the baby a little in that weird way, making goofy faces, but I think I lost my edge, babies usually go crazy, this one was not remotely interested, could be the beard, and m.) came home and wrote yesterday's yesterday, watched part of *Minnesota Clay* while you slept, took my pills, forgot the mask, observed our anniversary beginning at the last note of the day.

AUGUST 13, 2014

Yesterday I had no rituals. I showered and washed my hair but this is unusual. I chopped my hair some more. You helped me cut the back at an angle. It's only a little angle now, but someday it will be more. I slid oils all over my skin, probably too much because I got hot. I sweat through my coconut and vanilla oils.

Yesterday you gave me a massage because you left the burners on again. Someday we'll die by burner. Or our house is on fire and our children they will burn. I said you weren't going to cook anymore but we both know that's not going to happen. We psychoanalyzed your drive for death by burner. Out back eating oatmeal and chia seeds with fruits and nuts and hemp milk and a little agave and weak tea. Looking out at an expanse of desert and our trees, our little orchard of unnamed trees we don't know the names of.

You gave me a massage and I answered some important questions about anatomy. Your eyes look brighter against the beard. It's a five-month beard now, growing wide. I like the beard but I can't remember the face. I think you have an amazing chin under there.

Yesterday I cooked, which is rare, because you weren't allowed to touch the stove forever. Or a day. I made the rest of a bag of a fine Italian pasta, a gemelli. With mushrooms and squash and pepper and olive and avocado oils. It wasn't as good as if you made it. I was afraid I undercooked the mushrooms. They were meat. I always use too much oil. I want to make things taste good but I don't know how. I want to compete. I turn off the stove. I double-check. We get really full and I vow not to eat again.

You call an electrician with a French last name to come estimate the hot tub hookup. He doesn't come. You have to go to the Christians' house to pick up the enormous mangled used grandmother-gifted hot tub with six other guys. One is Scott, the handyman we found from Leafe, who asked for pictures of our place and I never sent them. I need to email Leafe.

We decide I can wait for the electrician while you go get the tub. This is rare. I stay home. I transcribe pages and pages from the pink notebook for parts of my new book, or it's another book, I can't decide. I can't read my handwriting. I hate my writing and then I decide it's genius. Who cares. I can't transcribe all the pages, it's too traumatic, there's too much. I write too much.

The electrician shows up late. Of course I'm on the toilet. I know that's when he'll come and when I come out of the bathroom, there he is. I let him in the gate. I keep the gate open. This is all rare. To let anyone in, to keep it open. He's stumpy and old and has gray teeth and either looks terrifying or nice. He has vaguely orthopedic sneakers and an impressive limp. He stands too close to me. There are a few times I imagine getting raped. I pick up a pink crystal looking stone and hold it in case. I check my phone a couple times, but don't want to be someone who checks her phone. The performance begins. The ultimate performance is being female alone in front of a strange man who is an electrician or a craftsman or a contractor or a workman of some kind. I keep my sunglasses on. I am suddenly high-pitched, small, delicate, and floral. I look at the ground. I wander slowly around while he makes measurements that mean everything will cost too much. He writes down the measurements in a floppy notebook. He is one of those electricians who tells you No every time you say something. He also questions the sensibility of every aspect of our house, including the two well tanks. He says things I don't understand and don't care about. He disagrees with every phatic comment I have, just trying to keep the channel open and not die.

-You all moved up here?
-Well we teach so we come up here on our free time, we get a lot of free time.
-No you don't.

A couple times I find my back is close to a wall or some other structure and he is leaning in with his gray teeth. He tells me his wife said they got a lot of rain today. He tells me about standing water in the road. At first I misunderstand and think he's complaining. He took the wrong road to get here. He goes into great detail about cutting wires on the house he's working on and how stupid everyone else is and how Edison won't come out to cut the electricity so he did it and how mad they'll be and he laughs. I nice along. But I know he's going to amp up the estimate. He asks for our number to call with the price, and I say here's my husband's cell phone. I say things like, That's not my forte, when showing him the two electrical boxes. I hate that part, but the performance has to go on, it's not my fault.

He leaves and you show up with Scott and the trailer and the hot tub in front, five guys in a jeep behind him, and you in the back in our VW station wagon. It took forever and I was imagining the hot tub on its side in a pickup pitching over the edge onto the highway. I tell Scott this afterwards. All these Christian guys are nice and strong and they laugh at my one joke and they don't want any beer. I've never met any guys moving anything before who don't want any beer. I've never met any guys before who don't want any beer. One guy apparently is wearing a t-shirt that says "I Love My Wife" and has a lot of Jesus shit on it, you tell me this later. I of course didn't notice that. I can't process people or their t-shirts. I tell you I'm going to make you wear a shirt like that when you're moving shit with guys sometime. Seriously I wonder if she made him wear that. I just can't fucking imagine what kind of people buy, wear, and move a hot tub in that kind of t-shirt. It's impressively awful.

We want to go see the James Brown movie but the times are no good. We want to go to Pappy's but it's closed Tuesdays. Natural Sisters closed at 7. We go to 29 Palms Inn where they grow their vegetables in a garden and we eat by the pool while an old white woman plays keyboards and an old white guy in a ponytail and, you guessed it, a loud printed short-sleeve button-down shirt and khakis, plays the trumpet really well and hand claps for the beat and sings like Louis Armstrong.

You eat a portabella mushroom and I eat a Caesar salad with too much cheese and tortilla strips. We animal a loaf of 200-year-old French starter sourdough and I eat two packets of butter hoping it's grass-fed but not really caring. I get a glass of pinot noir called Handcraft, which is ridiculous, and you get a glass of zinfandel and tell me it's sustainable, which is amazing, and I adore you.

A blond woman in a pink flesh—for pink flesh—colored string bikini with a short blond hair cut, all one length at her chin, gets in the pool. Her short white brunette man carries their adorable pixie-cut baby, a girl with only a waterproof diaper on. The woman holds the baby in the pool and swirls her around. The baby is giddy, the baby is so happy she is smiling, she is riding the pool, she is flying in water. She keeps very still with only a smile and large cheeks and her eyes are very wide. The man stays out of the pool and is an attendant or watches the musicians, who are next to him. We watch the baby. I watch the baby and you occasionally turn around to watch the baby when I tell you how cute it is. The woman and the baby get out and the man does a shaky dance with the towel and towels them off. They go to their room and come back later, all dressed. They sit at the table next to us when we're leaving, which means they eat dinner at 10, which means they're from Europe, as I figured. The baby throws her plastic bottle cap and eats a bowl of plain spaghetti while the couple orders steak, which is not available, then a sweet pork dish, which I wonder if they'll like, and a bottle of wine, which I admire. When we leave, I tell them they have a very good baby, because I can tell they're anxious about it and because the baby is pretty damn good. They both laugh as if they know how very bad the baby is, but grateful that someone thinks so.

We stop by Home Depot on the way back through the desert. On the way there, all the hills were pink and blue, babyish, and we listened to some news about Robin Williams but have to change the channel because it's too depressing and we talk about your cousin Julie's suicide and what's up with hanging and shouldn't you just get a boat and float out to sea and disappear or at least drive into the water on Fiesta Island with the windows closed, something a little more subtle and dignified. They're going to talk about children of suicides and so we change the channel but now I've got a headache and that sucks because the other guy from Big Star, not Alex Chilton, the Christian one, is on the radio and we want to hear it but I can't. At the Depot later, we get a clothesline and another magnetic door stop and you look for way too long at parts to hook up the refrigerator water. I'm silent but impatient. You're handy. Then I'm a woman waiting in the aisle at Home Depot and I consider sitting on a box and looking at my phone, but then you're done and we go home. We don't ring the bell for good customer service this time.

The dogs are so excited to see us today. I need to pet them more. I like to get on the floor with them but now I have a migraine and I just put on my striped pajama pants and a purple discount shirt and get in bed. You watch another Spaghetti Western and I sleep.

08.14.2014

Yesterday we had been married for nine years. We knew we were, the day coming was not a surprise. It has been a good life. We had made plans: Palm Springs for the night, staying at the Ace Hotel, which is made for us, our place, with its hipster camping aesthetic, cool with the dogs, but cheap enough now for the summer that we could actually stay there. We can go there and be a parody of ourselves, but everyone else is so extreme they barely look. We even saw someone there wearing my rare Bob Pollard t-shirt. We had a day before that though, the things one must do, typing yesterdays and doing the workout, the smoothies and the leftover rice and beans and the radio and the little chores of locking up, yahoo innoculation. Check-in was at 3 and that's about when we got there, they liked me because of my beard and my hat. There was a dog fee but no question about their size like it started to say on their website, it's an information deterent, but a place like this can't tell you no, especially in summer when you'd have to be crazy to go to Palm Springs. It was 112 something all day yesterday. We had dinner reservations at some place called The Workshop, which sources everything perfectly, and we felt healthy and familiar in our little patio room in the Ace, and I remembered that this is where you took some of your self-author portraits, right here, and I remembered how we copied a few of the things in both of our houses, we are the real homesteaders, but now our places were in better shape and the Ace needed a handyman. I could do it for them, but I have a job already. It was too hot for the dogs to be out of the room until later, so we went to the pool and positioned the shades so we couldn't get any sun, but even that was too hot so we swam for a while and went back to the shade then went back to the room. You reminded me of the time we were there before and we spent an hour rescuing bees from the water, carrying their stunned bodies in a handful of water to the safety of shore, keeping them far enough away from our palms so they wouldn't sting. We honored our union of nine years in many ways, no presents but the life we're building, which is plenty of present enough. You were real nice to me, but you always are, and I hope we weren't too much different yesterday than usual, but it's nice to have an excuse to privilege the relationship over all else. We went back to the room and found that of course the Ace gets TCM, which is the only channel we ever want to watch, and of course they had a Cary Grant day all day, which was cool because Cary Grant took acid when he acted and you can tell and of course I have a little part of me that wants to be the kind of man he is, the kind that would never be in a Western except for something execrably colonialist like *Gunga Din*, which isn't really a Western but whatever. There was one pre-code one where Cary Grant, who always of course plays Cary Grant, played a playboy who was interested in a poor working girl who was in love with a geologist and though she went to a party at Cary Grant's house and stayed late after she was almost raped by a society boy, they maintained their innocence even though he wore a kind of wizard robe, she caught a ride back with his driver and they didn't even kiss I think but everyone in town freaked the fuck out and all the ladies at the switchboards were talking about it to everyone in this shitty little town and it ruined the poor girl's life, she even got fired. Then the geologist came back after seven years or something and he was really tall but kind of awkward with the ladies, but he admitted this and it was charming and he didn't realize until later that the girl was going through this tough time and even though they were going to get married when he saw Cary Grant talk to her at a party he couldn't handle it. And it was still a surprise when the girl left with Cary Grant and didn't come home until the next day and they drove away to New York. The code ruined everything. We have been pre-code for ten years, really. We got dressed and you wore my favorite dress ever, the one I got you for your birthday in Maryland, crazy yellow, and you cut your hair and the flowers looked psychedelic around your perfect face. Your hair looked like the morning sun, just sneaking in the window. Cary Grant. We were hungry just in time and went to this Workshop place, which apparently has a chef who was an English graduate student but boy can he cook, and the restaurant is exactly where I want to live, a concrete church with isolation booths. We couldn't figure out what to order but by the time it was time we were full and had fries for our entree. There were other things before, a feast of salads and appetizers, but we were proud that we got so full on so little, and that we avoided the big beasts. Back at the Ace we were going to go to the bar but decided not to, we were so full and tired, so we lay on the bed and watched Cary Grant captain a submarine very capably, but Robert Osborne said that the set was actual size and they needed 30 costume changes for Cary Grant alone, what with the hot lights, and that tempers flared. It was a piece of complete racist patriotic trash, but that's the greatest generation for you. We both kind of slept through that one, though, then we took the dogs out and then we had our anniversary sex, which woke us up, and then there was another Cary Grant movie where he and his real wife and screen wife adopt troubled white kids, one had a bad attitude and one had leg braces, and they also adopted six cats, a dog, and a rabbit, though I may be forgetting something.

AUGUST 14, 2014

Yesterday we learned that Joey Ramone's real name was Jeffrey Hyman. While driving to Palm Springs listening to Bob Seger, the greatest rock lyricist of all time.

Yesterday nine years ago we were married in a field on a lake in Upstate or Western New York, depending on where you're from. Your little brother Brady played guitar in a tree. George Harrison. My mother cut tablecloths with shearing scissors out of lavender gingham cloth she had around. It was a public space and we occupied it. Lined up picnic tables and had our people claim them. Your sister Sarah strung the red paper lanterns and black and white umbrellas in the trees, which she told us was difficult. She gave us the reports on what everyone did and did not do, since we were somewhere else. You were getting into your green seersucker suit but you left the tighty whities in the van. My brother-in-law had to go get them. I didn't want to explain to him why they were essential, but they were essential. My sisters destroyed my hair and made me a monster, which is sort of what I wanted, but I had envisioned a more chic monster. MJ put green eye makeup on me, which matched Amit's shoes. My sister Janet took all the photographs since she's a professional, but apparently she lost all the film, black and white and color and somehow digital too, on the flight back to California, which happens. To her. So we have no evidence. We got married in silence on a mound of dirt in a circle and we were an hour late and we had grill boys dressed up like Ramones, grilling in the public park. Jay and Turco sang a gospel tune. Billy played steel drums. Susan and Chris and Jon read poems. My father made a toast, which I dreaded and was dreadful, but at least he didn't talk directly about virginity and your brand new ownership of my vagina. I think, I can't remember. We danced with an iPod remote in your seersucker pocket. I had the sleeves cut off of my mother's 1969 wedding dress, a high collar with white buttons all down the back. I wore green Prada shoes and you wore black and white Miu Miu boots, which we might have stolen. Cole and Toine danced like Fred and Ging. We took the keg back to the motel and Fuzzy had enough pot for everyone, even my sisters. We had a hot tub suite but we were too exhausted and drunk and you talked to too many people not me. We didn't want to waste paper or plastic so we had all glass dishes and silverware and the next day I washed it all, in the back field, in cold hose water, alone. My mother and sisters and everyone else inside. We drove off in the van and we couldn't wait to leave and my sister cried. I think we stopped in Cleveland.

Yesterday we went to the Ace for a night with Ronald & Kiki. This was Kiki's first hotel back when and we got a patio room again and I wonder if she remembers another time meeting her fans Joshua and Sarah here at Thanksgiving. Our room has a T. Rex record in it, but it's gone. I took an author photo here once you remind me. We plan to go to the photo booth in the lobby.

We go to a place called The Workshop for dinner. It's made of concrete and Edison bulbs and our appetites have shrank and I have a glass of rose prosecco that's not very bubbly but comes in a chilled curved cocktail glass. It must be 100 degrees at 8pm. Our waiter has a hair cut like a woman with short blond hair. We leave a cash tip.

We get TCM in our hotel room and I stay up watching it. You take a nap and then I wake you up again and we stay up half the night watching Cary Grant night, wrapping up with a picture starring him and his real wife and they have too many kids and they adopt more and they are black and white saints with excellent attitudes. They don't have sex, and this is a running punch line until the end.

FIVE

AUGUST 15, 2014

Yesterday was Charlie Chaplin day. One monkey takes off his pants, another bites his nose.

08.15.2014

Yesterday the sun, the new electrician, the missing negative, the aluminum roll, the lost friend text.

AUGUST 16, 2014

Yesterday I'm still wondering what you're writing about. This project may be ending since we dread and avoid it and it's almost a month. I'm not sure about the middle coda to my book, it's terrifying. I can't get away from reporting. We'll hear each other's yesterdays tomorrow at a reading at the Hideout. Just a few. Will yours be factual or true.

Yesterday we saw Jay Demko at the Casbah. He was down from Portland doing sound for a laptop-playing duo, an Australian five-piece Zappa–Peter Gabriel bit, and a "comedian poet." That's how he's billed. The Australian starts off the set by taking off his clothes, down to the boxers at least. I thought he might keep going. This is almost the best part. The whole time I'm worried that he might pop out the fly. Or I think maybe it's so small and tucked in or something. Later you tell me the shorts are sealed up. Does this mean you were worried too or that you were at least curious and looked.

Three large drunken aggressive seemingly-closeted possibly military men stand in front of us by the stage. I think I've seen them before and have had the same thoughts about them and wanted to stay out of their way. I see them every time. Can you have season tickets to a rock club? Are they my hallucination or projection?

The Australian, who is the son of Crowded House, says he wants to star in a magazine in praise of midsized men. Or is it medium sized. This is another good part. The chubby bass player takes off his shirt with delight. He doesn't look so chubby underneath. Some people look smaller without clothes. How judgy is this. Two girls sing at each side of the stage, one with a handheld pedal, one with a keyboard rig. They all sound at first like Boss Hogg, and then like Man Man, and then we walk around and talk to Ryan Hand and Demko.

The poet is giving a poetry reading in between sets, two sets, one to open and one in between. He has many books and CDs for sale from presses I never heard of. He has "national best seller" stickers added. Funny. He's not very funny. He's from Austin. All of his poem jokes seem to end with "and then I fucked her" or something. You quote me back to me saying poems are unmemorizable jokes.

I like Jay Demko. I like liking one of your old friends. He has two teeth in the front that meet at an angle. He reminds me of something. He has four kids and a lady. He is skinny with glasses and a grayish beard. He's not what I expected. He's much nicer than lots of guys, he looks me in the eye. Doesn't say anything that makes me want to kill. You tell me all about his ethics and his performances of self. He has a brother named Weed Hog, who I've heard about who is trying to be an actor in Eugene. He might take his kids to Legoland someday.

The Casbah is a familiar place. Demko asks if we go there much and we tell him yeah, but not so much lately. Then I blurt out the part about your cancer. We didn't discuss this but I figure it's rude not to tell him and Ryan Hand too. I am a woman in a group of boys doing a little emotional lifting. It's ok. I wanted to cut my hair again yesterday, but I ran out of time. I like the low lights in the back room by the pool tables. I like to watch the crowd. We walk around the block with the one-hitter.

Before the show, we get pizza in Little Italy. We scoot down on the red scooter through crazy traffic, or does it just seem crazy because we've been in the desert so long, or are all these people tourists. We scoot by my nephew's apartment and we need to see him, it's been a year maybe. Everyone has a baby or a pit bull. I suddenly get passionately interested in bassinets. Waiting at a stop sign, the cab right behind us gets rear-ended and flies forward. My emergency response tells you to go.

We sit outside and watch all the tourists or just bourgeoisie pushing their cute babies. We eat pizza and salad and wine.

When we go home, we take the scenic route by the park through the neighborhoods. We fall asleep watching last week's Buffalo Bills.

08.16.2014

Yesterday we packed up, we packed it in, got out of Dodge or Landers to be precise, I really awoke, because no movies at night, really awoke into the early almost cool morning, and did my exercise outside in the present, in the morning with the moon in front of me and the sun behind, did what was physically possible and attempted what was impossible, I increased my numbers, the dogs were loose and I knew you were sleeping and they began barking so fiercely I thought there was a person on the other side of the fence, but no, just the dogs hearing their things and adding to it. The hot tub had missing corners from the old owner's puppy and I wanted to cover them up because the electrician told me about pack rats that destroy these things, though they've probably been living in there for three years now, and now it will cost 2,000 dollars just to hook it up unless we move it which will involve more Christians, so I got scrap wood from the wood pile and worked early in the shade, but each corner required something different, I cut strips from a piece of plywood for two corners, after rejecting my first two plans, short scraps and the aluminum roll I bought the day before, and for the other, there was an old pallet I pulled apart. It looked good enough for something we'll never use. You came out and thought I shouldn't be out in the sun in just my cowboy hat and muscle shirt and nylon shorts, and though I was working in the shade, I didn't want you to think I don't care about my survival, and I do care about my survival, so I went inside and put a thick black sweatshirt on. Then I finished the job and was a little proud, you were doing yoga on the deck and I was proud to have a deck with you doing downward dog, and so I was still in a working mood even though I wanted to leave early to get a box from Ahsahta to drop off in time at the office for my tenure file, though you said that would never work and you were right in many ways, especially since the box never arrived, but anyway I drilled and screwed a padlock thingy onto our electrical box because the electrician told me that yahoos will come to your house and steal your wires which seems odd since they could steal all the rest of our stuff, but it was a good idea because at least it would hold the cover on, which was on the ground when we first inspected the place. You would have been proud of the care I took in not electrocuting myself, which I really could have done, but I want to have more days with you and I didn't tell you about how careful I was because some things must be spared until you hear about them in a yesterday and so I kept this present for you, this present called self-care, and then we got ready to go and did a few loads of laundry with our new machine and let things dry instantly in the hot wind and locked up and took our trash to the dumpster behind Kelly's Future which is the greatest name for a furniture store I can possibly imagine and lucky for us the dumpsters were unlocked and then we were really off. I drove us straight and we were here by three and on the way I noticed how the three-hour drive feels like the duration of an elevator ride, it's just the way to get somewhere, though the scenery is something, and though I missed my exit, we found another exit that was better because it was something new, even though we've done it before, and I noticed how different markers along the way had begun to find significance in me, the places where the arteries of traffic converged and you had to crawl but if you found the right lane, which was always the left, you had a chance. And we listened to the news for the first time in days and we heard about Michael Brown and Ferguson and Ron Johnson and I made some tears without even knowing they were coming. And we talked about race and cops but you can't I just can't and the word militarized should be the word of the year for sure like last year was selfie, and I drove carefully with rage in my body. And I told you about Jay who we were to meet yesterday night and how I was glad he texted me and told me he would be in town and how we hadn't spoken in nine years, but not for any reason at all, just because of inertia or maybe it was speed, but how I still wished him the best, him and his kids and Courtney, and how maybe of all my WV music friends, he was the one I wished the best to, and I tried to describe how things that annoyed me nine years ago now seemed like ok qualities, at least relatable, like his scrolling through identities, and how his dead dad had a lot to do with that, but he's been in Portland for nine years and what does that do to a guy who dropped out of junior high to break guitars, and I thought of our old bands, Kukim and Clubber Lang and the pomade and the $75 rent at Mesa House in Star City, about food stamps and tube amps and how I still think of it sometimes, and when we finally got home the house looked clean and sane from Delphine and we cleaned it more but we didn't have much time before we were to see Jay because he was running mix for two bands and one poet (?!) so we drove the scooter down to the Casbah but first to the Napizza, which I highly recommend, but San Diego was in some kind of summertime frenzy with tourists everywhere and there was an accident right behind us on the way but we scooted away alright, and we sat on the corner and ate our delicious roman organic pizza slices and our salad and watched more accidents, then I texted Jay and we met him in front of the Casbah and he was older and so was I, and the Hand was there too like a little '90s reunion and you told them right away that I had cancer and that killed the weird joy a bit until I smiled or did a little jig and Jay told me about his son who plays little kid football and loves to hit, and how all their kids go to private school even though their only job is Jay doing sound and Courtney fills out their applications and stays home with them, how they're always broke but if you stay at exactly zero you're ok, Jay said, you're better.

AUGUST 17, 2014

Yesterday I made note of some things.

We woke up late or we woke up early but got up late. First day back home in the big city, back with the internet. Looked at houses and neighborhoods online together just for fun. We don't want to move but we ogle domestic spaces. We see what a steal we got with a basement and a studio and a yard and a non-shithole.

I waited too long to feed the dogs. I made them some vegan mush to add to their kibble. If it's dry they eat anything. If it's wet, it has to taste good. I added coconut oil and nutritional yeast and flax and frozen veggies. Kiki is picky and skinny, Ronald has food aggression and desire issues.

We wanted to see City Heights so we went to the farmer's market. This is the cheapest farmer's market in town, everything's a dollar. No one is certified organic because it's too expensive and difficult, but they don't use sprays and we believe them. We stopped by the booth with the $15 bags and the vegan breakfast place with the veggie reuben. We got a brochure for an 8 year old girls' gluten-free vegan baked goods, all "thick and rich."

Things are diverse and varied and utopian at the market. We get a bundle of some green that looks like an herb or a weed. The woman tells us its name in Spanish, which we can't visualize or remember. She says it's like a spinach. A woman in a dashiki next to us looks skeptical and tells us No, shakes her head. Like she wouldn't get caught cooking with that weed.

We drove by the Waldorf School, which is the Rudolf Steiner school in town, which is the best bet if we had a kid. It's perched on a hill surrounded by gardens and a small café selling coconut waters. There's a blacktop and a basketball hoop, which you like. Everything is wood, which I like.

We went to Nate's Garden Café inside the City Farmers Nursery, where they sell organic plants and have chickens and baby goats. We heard about the baby goats over breakfast, which was at 2:00. You got a veggie reuben and I got a veggie hash scramble thing. Mine was basically a plate of potatoes in a skillet. Yours was just a slab of tempeh with a little sauerkraut. This seals the deal on eating out. I got a small Pellegrino because it's chilled and sparkly.

An older couple babies a dog behind you. They wipe the dog's mouth. It's an older German Shepherd and I have an innate fear response.

Two tables of loud couples of friends behind and beside us. One blond woman walks away to talk on her phone at the other end of the patio. She seems to be driving things. The men look military. Are they happy at all. One woman's personality is bigger than everyone else's. They all drink beer, or most of them.

An enormous man with sleeve tattoos walks into the restaurant carrying a huge sack over his shoulder, followed by a scruffy blond child and a woman with a long ponytail, knee socks, '80s terrycloth shorts, a tank top. She looks cheerleader-ish. Until I notice the face tattoos. She has tattoos all over her neck and onto her cheek and on her nose and up to her eyes. I think this is probably child abuse. They walk out moments later without the sack. The woman says something to the kid to come on, she sounds nice and I get a look at the kid who has almost white hair and scars and scabs on his face.

We buy some arugula seeds and some basil seeds, two kinds of each. You get a bag of topsoil to add to our compost. You're going to give this growing thing a shot.

Then we drove home the wrong way down Home Ave. and up through South Park for fun. We pulled over when you saw the sign for the electronics guy. He is in a garage with '80s and '90s and newer electronics spilling out onto the sidewalk. He has no front teeth, wears a white t-shirt and is pretty hard to understand. Did he say the electronic drum kit was only $30? He tells us to play it. He has some jazz on the record player but he puts on a Roy Orbison. I play the drums. Then I tell you to play the drums. He tells us to hit it harder. Then he plays the drums. We all play the drums to "Pretty Woman." You're bummed because he doesn't have any good gear.

The rest of the day is sleepy and getting ready to see the Sonics at the church down our street with Kylie and Brett. I do yoga and you do your crazy workout in the basement. We watch the Buffalo Bills play Pittsburgh and lose at the end by three. I text Ronaldo, I wonder where he is. He said something about packing up back east.

I cut my hair again and again. I shower outside and wash my hair but I use too much conditioner so I have to rewash it because it's a greasy pile. I use a hairdryer for the first time in years.

We walk to the coffee shop to meet Kylie and Brett who are sitting in the back. It feels like more than two or three weeks since we've seen them. Maybe it's a month, maybe since right before the yesterday project. Maybe we don't see people enough.

The Sonics rock the shit out of the church. We all get our eardrums blown.

My favorite spot on the side of the stage is shit for ears.

We all devise our band, which is actually a troupe called the North Park Slashers, based on my desire to stab myself in the butt every time I see that poster for the new gym—two tiny white teenage asses in terrycloth gym shorts. We say we should go around slashing asses, really let the cheeks dangle.

Kylie and Brett have the same anniversary as we do. Lucky 13.

08.17.2014

Yesterday around 8, not so bad. Yesterday looking at schools on Redfin, looking at houses in bed with you. Looking inside the houses on my iPad. Wondering where we would fit another one of us. In bed all morning, looking at houses and looking at the Waldorf School, then the other charter school with Waldorf principles. You didn't like that one as much, they mentioned the Common Core. Yesterday in bed. The Waldorf School in City Heights, where the kids learn to weave and make their own costumes. Where they don't believe in tests, where they do eurythmy. Yesterday cutting your hair everyday. Yesterday looking down at my angry scar. Driving to City Heights to make it by one to try the farmer's market there. The world's cheapest farmer's market. City Heights neighborhood of all neighborhoods. City Heights holiness of tortilla shops, of tower bar, of injera, of spring rolls and City Heights. And now, the best small farmer's market around, where even Susie's Farm will not venture, but where the bike co-op fixes bikes and the hummingbird makes vegan treats from the other farmer's wares and a little girl with an amazing name sells gluten-free sweets from her menu, and everything is listed as thick and rich. O City Heights where kale costs a dollar, everything costs a dollar. Where these cool kids will put together a bag of vegetables for you for fifteen dollars. We were entranced there, bought something from almost everyone, put tips in the baskets where we couldn't find anything to buy. Then to the Waldorf, where we parked and it was Saturday, which was a good thing and we imagined where another of us would go to school, we looked at her view into the infinitude of San Diego, and I watched you looking, and we saw the book they were all reading, a book about the perils of sports in schools on the young psyche, and yes this was the place that we would make a baby for. We peeked over the fence, I held you up to look over another. And we drove a little further to the incredible garden supply spot and to Nate's Garden Grille for breakfast at 2, and it was positively terrible, but all locally grown, and it was fine because it verified that we must fend for ourselves in this world, all of our selves and our little one, and Ronald Johnson and Kiki Smith, who we belong to as much as they belong to us. And I bought seeds to grow and we looked at the baby goats sleeping on their mother. And homeward and I did so much laundry, I dried it all in the sun and took it down as soon as it was dry and folded it on the line, all the sheets that Delphine and her wonderful family from France used, they had stripped the sheets before they left, her children had, and now I was putting them in the sun and sea breeze and they smelled like baby heads. Exercise and laundry and good ole time time. Every yesterday I might not have had. Should I feel sad? Should I be grateful? And I made some lentil mush in the pressure cooker and some rice in the pan and we knew we would need to eat it fast because we were walking down the streets to see the Sonics with Brett and Kylie and we'd already bought them tickets because we knew they loved the Sonics and because we have money and they are poor graduate students and we met them at the coffee shop on the way for tea and found out we have the same anniversary even though they're not married but they're sweet little anarchists and we found out that Brett bought a camera and a recorder and is going to go back to Ohio and get the frackers on tape. And we acted silly with our antioxidant teas, mine was hot and yours was iced, iced saint tea, you're a saint for sure, in some other kind of system, though, something higher, and we acted positively silly with these people a little younger than us, they were healthy and so were we, we talked about juice, we invented a new band called the North Park Slashers that project images of wounds on sexist racists, and we went to the Irenic, which is a church where they have concerts, and Kylie said they hadn't been to a concert in ever, only when they get in for free like when

Brett played shows and I thought a little about what money is, it's money, money, money, and you and I can't stand the opening band so we stood in the smoking lounge and said more crazy stuff but the Sonics came on a little later and they were older than anyone but they had survived to play their one brilliant song for an hour.

AUGUST 18, 2014

Yesterday we didn't know how it would go. Reading our yesterdays at the Hideout to the San Diego poets, our friends. You sat on the couch and I sat in the blue chair with our laptops and we read all our yesterdays, to ourselves. We sat there for hours. We timed one. Maybe they are not meant to be read in one sitting. Maybe they are meant to be read together. We still didn't share ours with each other. We stuck to the yesterday gag.

In the morning we collaborated on two scrambled eggs with red pepper, zucchini, that fake spinach that looks like a weed, basil, and brown rice. I wanted us to eat a plum but we got too full. We ate out back in the shade under the pergola surrounded by butterflies and flies.

We proofed our yesterdays then we walked the dogs around the block. I walked Kiki and she wasn't so bad. I let her walk ahead of me so she thought she was walking with you and Ronald. They both took big shits in the park and you scooped it up. I wonder if you talk about that in your yesterdays, how you do all the scooping. I still don't know because I only heard three of your yesterdays. I feel bad that you still do all the scooping but I don't even know if you want me to do the scooping. Maybe if I do diapers that will be evener.

I do know that your yesterdays sound like you. And they sound like our days. And they also sound like me too. Maybe they're not as different as I imagined they would be, not as gendered or separated egg whites. But the differences matter and it's these spaces that define the thing, us. The ongoing relationship experiment as we used to say. I just typed relationshop which seems better.

At first we were going to read three yesterdays and then the two short ones, but maybe the short ones are just novelty yesterdays, so we decide on four regular sized ones. One from the early part in Mendocino, two from the desert, and one from San Diego with people in it. I'm excited to hear yours.

We decide not to do Pilates. There's no time. I pick out a dress for the reading, a short coral blue lace fabric with an underlayment like a floor. It didn't used to fit me so well before our cancer diet. I wear my new used buttercream boots. My silver heart earrings that I got in 8th grade in 1988 from Antonia "Sweetie" Stout whose sister was named Chicken. Yes, they were millionaire heiresses. I don't think she gave them to me, but I still have them. My common law silver heart earrings.

You go with your new black Levis that fit and my favorite white snap down collar shirt with the green clover circles. But then you change for a black t-shirt with a V. Then I say I like the collared shirt. But you're worried about getting hot and sweat and so you try on a short sleeve collared shirt, a hip little thing that at first I think is too tight because it used to be too tight, but now it fits just fine. You wear that. You like how "flexible" my hair is, you say it's the perfect 1960s do.

We get to the Hideout and it's awkward to talk to people without being drunk. There are a lot of spaces in the talking. We haven't seen everyone for months. You don't try to fill the gaps too much. I try but not too hard. Tina is kind and gentle and warm. I like her sweater and her haircut. She likes my haircut. Someone calls it asymmetrical, which is news to me, but since we chopped it together maybe this is accurate.

I want to go sit with Rae and Chuck, who are sitting in a booth at the front with Gabe. Everyone is here or coming here. We saw Keith walking over crossing the street wearing his favorite black t-shirt with some yellow thing on it, which is probably some superhero or game character he told me about but I can't remember. I think I remember it's his favorite.

Chuck shows us pictures of an incredible mushroom. Everyone watered their garden so much while they were in Italy that their tree grew out of control and made mushrooms. I ask if they'll eat them, but they're probably lethal.

I recognize this is not very funny or entertaining. What I really want to tell about is being on stage together, each with our own microphone, reading our yesterdays out loud. The lights were bright and hot and I couldn't see anyone. Your yesterdays were funny and true. I skipped part of mine. We only read three each which took 18 minutes, so I stopped us short of the fourth. I said, There's more. You said, A whole month! At the beginning I said they might be boring. At the end Rae said they weren't boring. You told me later mine had style, which I didn't know. I thought yours had style too, but I loved your prose and hearing you write without the sound guide. We agreed that these are pieces without armor of sound or tricks. We're trying to face shit. Facing isn't easy.

Yours weren't all about movies and I was surprised a little. We both mentioned the three wall ovens and Gary Cooper and Leonard Cohen and lots of Ronald & Kiki. We said later that one memory shared by two people is definitely a memory. Otherwise, who knows.

People seemed to like our yesterdays, or they were glad to see us and concerned, or both or a mixture. Adam Veal and Brad Flis and Steve Willard were there, though Steve missed the reading, he just got back from teaching in China, he had some sharp words about the Ferguson situation, which were good words in solidarity. Gabe and Nicolee and new poets

Sarah and Chris from Oakland and Brett and Angela the poetry operative, and Kiik A-K and Hanna and Keith and Grant and Tina and Ryan and Sarah showed up just in time and sat at a front table. Mark Wallace was there and I talked to him in one burst. Ana Carrete gave her fare thee well reading from a blue bag on her shoulder with her chapbooks and then an iPad in a leopard print mini skirt and high heel black ankle boots. Theron and Kimmy read too, and Tina did a selfie spell, and Grant read his billion dollars piece, for us and not for us. Pepe came up from Tijuana. We want to see all these people again and again. We want to see them all at the desert or at our house or for a one-on-one. Will there be time.

We liked not being in charge of anything. We liked not getting fucked up. I don't know how to write these yesterdays anymore. Is this the last one or a sort of coda. Do I really know what a coda is?

We left before the karaoke got kicking, but not before we heard Stephanie belt out something amazing with hand gestures, some pop song about doing it I didn't know. Her man Nate sang Tom Waits, a bold move and nicely done. Then Tina, who we were waiting for, sang No Doubt's "What's Going On" and we could hear her from outside. Then we went inside to hear better, of course she was incredible. Then we went back outside and got smoked on and left. We planned to go to Tijuana to see Pepe. We planned a Brad Flis party where we'll all listen to Leonard Cohen in the desert and talk about Canada. We need to get a futon, we have a few tents.

When we came home the dogs were too excited, pretty bad in fact, Kiki jumping high and in circles, which would work for a Jack Russell but not a pit. You were starving and we made some bread a guest had left in the freezer even though it has a little sugar. You toasted us each a slice with coconut butter and NuttZo, your favorite Brazil nut butter. We ate the plum. You said it tasted like cake. We watched Charlie Chaplin's *The Kid* in bed. You fell asleep without any melatonin. I connected the dots on the narrative.

08.18.2014

Yesterday we knew we would hear each other's yesterdays. There was a reading that evening at this place the Hideout amongst the little scene we've helped gather. I hadn't heard a word of yours, and I hadn't looked back at mine. We spent the day reading them—our own pieces only, and I had to have your help matching the days with their labels. The dates are the days they are written, not the days we are talking about, and somehow this simple fact was too complicated for me. But you were patient as always, and now I have a permanent excuse. I was nervous to see people, we've been bivouacked elsewhere most of the time, little human contact except here in our real home, not wanting to talk about it, not wanting to explain. There was a heaviness to reading the pieces, some memory of them, lots of judgment:

So often during the process I resented the process that I would rush them, just try to get the pages down before I could do something else far from my mind. And it had been a month: just some writing each day for a month, just a way to get back into it, into rituals I have never had, clarity, honesty, and maybe even something good for me, I think maybe this was your idea, to get me to meditate a little more to be a little more here while I am still here. In Chinese medicine you deal with the terrain, and my terrain has been cleansed physically, but in Chinese medicine the terrain includes one's psychology and all disease happens for a reason. Was it my head, my heart, or my mouth that got us here? Was it the fields around the devices? I'm sure it was all of them, and the sunburn when I was a baby. But I still love you, sun. I remember at the Integratron when the sun came streaming from the sky during the soundbath, cut across my face, down my chest and settled on my scar. We made amends, the sun and I. We made a bio for our part of the reading that said we lived here and in the desert. It is true. We've lived lots of places, in Ohio, in Denver, LA, in that crazy cabin in West Virginia where we were snowed in and Ronald plowed a path through the snow so we could walk out into the beautiful. In Virginia, in DC, in Maryland, in a tent, in Canandaigua, in a hundred apartments we always unpack everything into. But we live in these two places now, and I'm going to be alive with you for a long time, and it will be here. We will have the beach and the sand. And I was reading my yesterdays and thinking of yours and what could they be like? Would I be revealed as the shame I am? Would your nondenominational saintliness put things in relief forever: I don't deserve you. But no one deserves anyone. And I read mine and thought a little about what the audience would need to know from them, and knew that we would work it out, we could try any. We would get through it. And it was just a little reading with six other readers, but it felt significant, I could see you a little nervous as well, you said so yourself. And I read on about the things we had done, poor us with no work to do, with nothing but time and movies and music and it was clear that that was a job too. It is a job to live. And I didn't feel sorry for anything, I felt like it was you and I and we were okay as long as we were both in the same place. And I couldn't believe my writing, not because it was good or bad, but because it had a subject and I have been an enemy of subject, because it wasn't driven by sound because that is where I thought the truth was. And even now, I cringe a little at the word truth, I would have never used such a word before yesterday, but now I do it all the time, already twice in the last two sentences. And we chose four days for little reason and we went to the Hideout and our people were there, or they got there, Rae and Chuck and Tina and Grant and Gabe and Pepe and Adam and Hanna and Keith and we were sitting in the corner and more people came in like Brad and the Hand and Sarah and Mark and Brett came in and Ana was there and someone familiar looking who I later met and told us my condolences and Adam told him that was not the right phrase to use and Steve showed up later after it was all over, and these two new poets who had moved to town, Sarah and Chris, and I ordered us two ice waters and there were other people I didn't know and they kept coming in and they were our friends and we listened to a few readers I didn't know but had heard read before and their work was wonderful and another reader from St. Louis was in town and I didn't get her name but her work was wonderful and Tina read and she made a spell for everyone with incense and selfies and Ana brought the incense sticks my way but couldn't light them but I could and there was smoke around us and we took a selfie of the two of us and we looked like we had been through a lot but we were through it and then it was intermission and I had to pee but both bathrooms in the hideout were occupied so I stood and listened to the ambulances rushing by and then it was time for us to go up and read our yesterdays together.

Ben Doller's most recent book is *Fauxhawk* (Wesleyan University Press); Sandra Doller's most recent book is *Leave Your Body Behind* (Les Figues Press). They live in San Diego and Joshua Tree with a baby and a pit bull named Wild Alphabet and Kiki Smith. They teach for California.

SIDEBROW BOOKS | www.sidebrow.net

ON WONDERLAND & WASTE
Sandy Florian
Collages by Alexis Anne Mackenzie
SB002 | ISBN: 0-9814975-1-9

THE COURIER'S ARCHIVE & HYMNAL
Joshua Marie Wilkinson
SB010 | ISBN: 0-9814975-9-4

SELENOGRAPHY
Joshua Marie Wilkinson
Polaroids by Tim Rutili
SB003 | ISBN: 0-9814975-2-7

FOR ANOTHER WRITING BACK
Elaine Bleakney
SB011 | ISBN: 1-940090-00-8

NONE OF THIS IS REAL
Miranda Mellis
SB005 | ISBN: 0-9814975-4-3

THE VOLTA BOOK OF POETS
A constellation of the most innovative poetry evolving today, featuring 50 poets of disparate backgrounds and traditions
SB012 | ISBN: 1-940090-01-6

LETTERS TO KELLY CLARKSON
Julia Bloch
SB007 | ISBN: 0-9814975-6-X

IN AN I
Popahna Brandes
SB013 | ISBN: 1-940090-02-4

SPED
Teresa K. Miller
SB008 | ISBN: 0-9814975-7-8

VALLEY FEVER
Julia Bloch
SB014 | ISBN: 1-940090-03-2

BEYOND THIS POINT ARE MONSTERS
Roxanne Carter
SB009 | ISBN: 0-9814975-8-6

To order, and to view our entire catalog, including new
and forthcoming titles, visit www.sidebrow.net/books.